OF DONUTS, TOILET PAPER, GRACE, AND LOVE: A LIFE IN MINISTRY
Volume One

Don Robinson

Prevenient Publishing
Mill City, Oregon

Front and Back Cover Photos:
By C.J. Robinson

OF DONUTS, TOILET PAPER, GRACE, AND LOVE:
A LIFE IN MINISTRY
Volume One

Chapter Titles

Introduction

OF DONUTS, TOILET PAPER,
GRACE, AND LOVE:
A LIFE IN MINISTRY
Volume One

Dedicated to Danny, Leon, and Scott who showed the way.

Introduction

The stories in this book are true – mostly. They all reflect actual people involved in real events; however, on occasion I have combined people and events that were separate. Of course, all names have been changed. Conversations are not word-for-word transcriptions; I didn't write them down at the time of their occurrences, so they are re-constructed, sometimes with embellishments. Some of Pastor John's reflections and observations came long after the events but are reported herein as contemporaneous. Further, although events occurred at different churches, no attempts are made to draw the distinctions.

My purpose in writing this volume is somewhat selfish. It is an attempt to personally reflect on and make sense out of fifteen years in pastoral ministry with The United Methodist Church. For me, it's a summing up, a report of things done and lessons learned. For the reader, I hope that the stories teach an important lesson about the church and about God: Amid conflict, chaos, and seeming triviality, God is working and the church accomplishes; donuts and toilet paper do matter and the ways in which we deal with them are indicative of how we view the kingdom of God. For clergy, especially new pastors, maybe the lessons learned by Pastor John will help them avoid making the same mistakes; then they can be free to make their own original mistakes.

It is my desire that there be a few chuckles in here. So much of what we humans do is hilarious even though we often don't intend it that way. I truly believe that God must spend much time laughing at the drama we put on.

Finally, I want to thank the people of The United Methodist Church for allowing me to be one of their pastors. I am grateful to all the characters in and out of this book who gave me inspiration, joy, sorrow, headaches, and oodles of love as I strove to work out my calling; through all of them, I've experienced the presence of God over and over. Specifically, I thank my wife Carol who faithfully lived these stories with me, and Mary Jane Peterson-Frazier of Hampton, Illinois, an angel who diligently read and critiqued all the drafts and provided encouragement to keep writing.

May God's Holy Spirit be present in the reading of these words as she was in the writing.

Chapter 1

The Donut War

Let me tell you a tale of donuts. Yes, donuts -- those deep-fried, jelly-filled, crème-infused, sprinkle-coated, nut-encrusted confections that are a staple of American culture and holy and sacred to the church. This sacramental understanding grows out of years stickily spent as a pastor striving to ascertain the spiritual state of those church-going people collectively referred to as congregations. That said, I begin the tale in earnest.

The meeting went awry at the very outset – even before it began. First, Judy, the finance chair-elect, forgot to attend and Pastor John had to place a desperate call to her just as the session was due to commence, for she was, he thought, a truly reliable advocate for his vision of what the church ought to be. (Her forgetfulness would have ramifications beyond the meeting; it would later provide Ted Fish with ammunition with which to rail at the pastor for his poor judgment on financial matters.) Second, Bob, the current chairperson, desired to project an Excel spreadsheet on a screen so all could see the proposed budget figures as they were plugged in; this necessitated holding the session in the sanctuary where face-to-face interaction was difficult. In this manner, the stage was set for the pillar of Reason to be knocked out of John Wesley's venerable Quadrilateral approach to decision-making. So, in keeping with the bizarre dynamics of meetings – church and otherwise – the rational folks became irrational and the irrational became out-of-this-world crazy.

"Okay," Bob began, "the figures from the stewardship campaign are in, so we have a projection for next year's income. Now let's go through the budget item-by-item, plugging in the committees' requested funds for ministry and the anticipated fixed expenses for next year."

"It's a waste of time," Ted Fish interjected. "We already know it won't balance."

"But we need to see exactly how much and in what ways the expenses exceed expected revenue," Pastor John pointed out. "And so does the church council; it's the body that determines the priorities. Don't forget, we can also propose ways to raise additional revenue."

"Why are we here if we can't make the decisions?" Ted countered. "Let's just go home."

Ahh, home, Pastor John thought. If he called Jean and said the meeting was over, supper could be close to ready by the time he got there. And then he'd have some time later to wrestle with the Gospel reading for Sunday's message. He also began to daydream about how peaceful his former life as a trial attorney seemed in retrospect. In the courtroom, the judge would rule and the petty squabbling would have to cease. In a committee setting, however, anyone could take it into his head to try to be the final arbiter of all things secular and spiritual. At this point, John was perfectly happy to drop the whole matter and tell the church council on Monday that the finance committee and its Pharisees had failed to come up with a proposed budget, balanced or unbalanced. The arrival of Judy broke into his reveries and dragged him back to the unpleasant reality of the present.

"Okay, let's start at the top," Bob said, ignoring Ted and hoping to get some cooperation. "Apportionments."

Ted: "Cut 'em in half,"

Pastor: "We can't. The conference dues are fixed and we are obligated to pay them as a member church of the denomination."

Ted: "Why do we have to be a part of the denomination? Let's pull out."

Pastor: "That decision is hardly within the purview of this committee."

Ted: "Then let's just all go home."

Pastor John thought back on his seminary classes that dealt with church polity and administration. In light of all he had been taught there, would it be appropriate to say at this point, "No, Ted, we're not all going to go home, but I strongly suggest that you pack up your stuff and get out of here as quickly as you can."?

"Sunday School," Bob courageously continued.

"Cut it by a third," Ted said. "They can re-use some of the old curriculum. They don't have to keep buying that new stuff. In fact, they should just use the Bible; we have lots of those around. They could take the ones in the pew racks 'cause no one looks at them anyway."

Maybe I could get my law license reinstated, Pastor John thought fleetingly.

Judy, her exasperation clearly showing, spoke up, saying, "Look, Shari, as Children and Youth Director, has given us a very detailed request for her ministry and I think we need to give it the respect and consideration it deserves."

"My question," Ted blurted out, "is: 'Why all the nit-pickin' detail?' We don't care about any of that. Just give her the money and let her decide how to spend it. That's what I do at home. I just give my wife the money and tell her she's got to feed us for a month with it. I don't try to specify how many eggs she buys."

"I think," Pastor said, "that what Shari is trying to do is to show us and the church council how her request is grounded in the mission and vision of the church. It's not just a random amount. I believe this is a good thing."

A new voice arose out of pew number six: "I'd like to know what you claim on your income taxes, Pastor, as to the rental value of the parsonage. You know that's a benefit and you have to pay taxes on it."

John's head was spinning with the growing incongruity of the conversation. Was this last query an attempt to open up the Pastor-Parish Relations Committee's recommendation as to pastoral compensation? Additionally, the question certainly blurred his focus with a new level of anxiety because he wasn't entirely sure his tax preparer was dealing with the issue properly. (He later ascertained that his accountant had indeed correctly followed the law.)

"Wait a minute," Bob mercifully interposed. "What are we going to do with Sunday School?"

"Cut it in half," Ted asserted, reducing his own earlier recommendation.

The ship was setting sail. Everyone began to jump on board – Treasurer, Finance Secretary, Trustee Chair. "Cut it!" they bellowed in a call and response pattern Pastor John wished he could get them to replicate in Worship on Sunday mornings.

Pastor John tried once again. "It's not this group's job to decide on ministries. Your task is to assemble data on expenses and ministry area funding requests and to estimate revenue. The council will determine the priorities if there is a revenue shortfall, and it could ask this committee to develop some additional fundraising approaches."

"Don't we have to present the council with a balanced budget?" Ted shot back.

"No," John said unhesitatingly.

"Judy, what do you think as incoming finance chair?" Bob inquired.

Judy reflected for a moment, then affirmed Ted's assertion. "Yes, we need to give the council a balanced budget."

It was over. Nothing meaningful was going to come out of this meeting. Jesus hadn't even been mentioned, but as the leader of the church he was being crucified again. John knew that a good story was needed. Jesus would share a parable in such a situation. Abraham Lincoln would spin a yarn. But Pastor John couldn't think of a thing.

"Okay, Sunday School's cut in half," Bob declared. "How about Missions?"

"We've gotta pay our lights, heat, salaries, landscaping, snow removal before we consider any money for missions," Ted announced. "We know we haven't got enough to do even that, so cut Missions out totally. Delete it."

"Such an action would certainly be contrary to the policy we adopted as a church several years ago," John began.

"Policies are made to be changed!" Ted intoned in what he surely thought was a prophetic-sounding and wisdom-laden voice.

Bob: "OK, what's the thought on Missions?"

Ted: "Zero. We need to be doing more for the people right here -- in our own town."

Sally: "Cut it by half."

June: "50% reduction."

Ken: "Reducing by half sounds good to me."

Judy: "Increase it from 7% to 8% of the budget. It's the church's goal to keep upping mission dollars until we get to a full tithe going outside the church." (Yes! Judy, John thought. You're back to your old self.)

Bob: "It seems a 50% reduction reflects the majority opinion pretty well. That's what we'll put down. Now how about Donuts, currently at $1400?"

"$1400!" Ted exclaimed. "That's absolutely absurd. How can we possibly spend that much on donuts?"

"Well," Pastor John spoke up, "our donut order runs about $22 each Sunday. Multiply that times fifty-two and you come up with $1144. Occasionally we order extra for special events and when we expect a larger than normal crowd on Sunday. So, $1400 is pretty much in line with reality."

Everyone seemed to think that spending $1400 annually for an unhealthy item was probably unwise. Judy proposed asking members of the congregation to bring healthier treats for the fellowship time and her suggestion seemed to meet with silent consensus.

"Alright, strike Donuts from the budget," Bob announced.

The meeting continued in the same vein, cutting drastically those items not related to building maintenance and salaries until anticipated income equaled budgeted expenses. While the bottom line looked good, the mission of the church was in financial shambles.

Following the meeting, Pastor John apologized to Chairman Bob. "Sorry, Bob, I wasn't prepared. I should've seen that coming, but I didn't give it enough thought. There was no sense of community in this group tonight. Somehow we kept the Holy Spirit out of the circle, and everyone just went their own way. It's my job to keep us focused and I just didn't do it. What you experienced tonight were two visions of church thrown into competition. One sees church as God's instrument for making a difference in the world, for transforming the world if you will, by engaging the world with God's love as shown in Jesus; it's an outward-looking vision focusing on those outside the church. The other sees church as existing for the benefit of its members, caring for them and meeting their needs; it's an inward-looking vision. Although I favor the first, I know there must be both. They really are not in competition."

As John walked home, he finally thought of an appropriate story he should have shared with the committee: The story in Numbers of the twelve guys Moses sent to scout out the settlement possibilities in Canaan. Ten of them came back in great fear of the people they found there, and their fear permeated the people of Israel and prevented them from moving forward into God's purposes.

The folks on the committee were scared. They were scared by the giant monster of not enough money. They had all grown up in a culture where there never seemed to be enough money to do all the good that needed to be done or even to do the bare minimum called for. Doing good was always something to be financed out of surplus and there never seemed to be much, if any, surplus. They forgot that God was with them and that when you're doing what God wants, nothing can stop you. They forgot. And Pastor John failed to remind them.

Thankfully, John was better-prepared spiritually for the church council meeting and many of the drastic cuts suggested by Ted and friends were tempered. However, donuts remained on the chopping block, and Judy's idea of volunteer donations of apples, oranges, veggies, and the occasional cookie gained acceptance.

It wasn't long before Pastor John (still smarting from the finance committee meeting) had the brilliant idea of stopping the donut supply at once rather than waiting for the beginning of the new budget year. Might as well start saving immediately, he thought. So, he promptly asked Mary, the church secretary, to call the donut shop and cancel the church's standing order. He informed the fellowship team of the need to begin alternative arrangements immediately.

The first Sunday without donuts dawned, and there were apple slices, orange slices, a veggie tray. This is going to work, John thought to himself as he surveyed the arrangement.

But then there was little Joey.

After Sunday School Joey marched into the fellowship hall in high expectation of his donut treat.

But there were no donuts.

Joey stopped, studied the situation for a moment, then let out an agonized howl and began sobbing.

Ted, of course, was right there peering out from his Sunday School classroom which was adjacent to the fellowship hall.

Joey's mother assured Judy who was one of the servers that it really wasn't a problem. Joey had been having an "off" day from the moment he got up. He just wasn't up to dealing with any change on this day. He'd be fine next Sunday.

But Ted would hear none of it.

For Ted, it was a disaster.

On Monday Ted confronted Pastor John. "We've got to have donuts for the kids!"

"There were lots of treats," John countered.

"It has to be donuts!"

"Nothing but donuts will do?"

"Nope. The kids have to have donuts. They were literally crying for the donuts on Sunday for God's sake!"

"But we took them out of the budget."

"Just delegate, Pastor! Simply tell the fellowship committee to get donuts. Let them figure out how. Communicate what you want and expect them to be creative enough to get it done. That's true leadership."

From then on donuts were funded.

The church had spoken: A world full of children without food to eat is tolerable. Not so a lack of donuts for church kids.

Chapter 2

Toilet Paper Battles

No sooner had the donut war ended than the toilet paper battles began.

They began with Ted Fish's announcement that for health reasons he would no longer be able to manage the church's toilet paper and paper towel needs. Ted's stepping-down was understandable. His decreasing mobility due to a variety of physical ailments had made the task a doubly arduous one for him – first in going to the stores to acquire the items and second in traipsing all over the church to deliver the supplies to the appropriate locations. Physically, he just couldn't handle it any longer.

Ted had originally gotten wrapped up in the paper business when he unilaterally decided it was improper to expect Ron Weaver to do it all. Ron wasn't very happy about it, but at Ted's insistence, Ron and Ted took turns assuming the responsibility by alternating weeks. Ultimately, Ron became unable to participate, and Ted went solo. The church was ready to reimburse costs, but Ron had rarely made a claim and, apparently, did not inform Ted of the availability of the funds. Shortly before he resigned, Ted learned of his right to reimbursement and became quite indignant that he had not been previously advised of it; accordingly, Pastor John endured another one of Ted's rants about the deplorable way in which church business was administered on John's watch.

With Ted's stepping-down, the church was faced with two issues: First, finding someone to take on the physical aspects of the job; second, paying for it. Stimulated by the volunteerism effort in the donut arena, Pastor John thought maybe such an approach would work in the paper supply area. God provided manna and quail for God's people in the desert; maybe God's people today would supply toilet paper to God's church. Members of the congregation could bring in the paper, deposit it in a designated location, and the custodian, the office staff, and he could get it distributed. He'd run an announcement/solicitation in Sunday's bulletin.

As soon as he got home for lunch he ran the idea by his wife Jean. To characterize her reaction as skeptical would be to grossly understate it.

"Are you crazy?" she asked with that I-can't-believe-you're-even-considering-it look on her face.

"That's not the way they do things here. The people aren't going to want to bring toilet paper to church."

"I think some of them would. It's a way to give to the church other than by putting money in the offering plate."

"But you're going to keep pressing them to put money in the plate. 'Tithe and then go beyond the tithe' is your mantra. I think they're going to say, 'We've paid generously into the church treasury; the church ought to be able to supply toilet paper.'"

"I think you're wrong, Jean."

"Remember what happened to Pastor Dave over in Highland?"

"No."

"He asked for help mowing the parsonage yard because it was so large. It was huge – and much of it on a hillside."

"Oh, yeah."

"They took him a used lawnmower and told him to have at it. It wasn't even self-propelled."

"That was pretty funny."

"Pastor Dave didn't think so."

"Well, he did end up losing some weight."

"Sue was sure he was going to have a heart attack every time he mowed – more because of how mad he got than from the exertion. She said he'd come in sputtering and fuming just like that old lawn mower. You don't want to end up like that, do you?"

"No, but – "

"The point is that a pastor has to recognize the church culture and attempt to operate within it wherever possible. Pastor Dave should've taken bids for mowing contractors and then asked for the church to pay a part of the cost. That's the way they do things there. You just need to find someone to replace Ted and prepare to pay for the supplies. You run that piece in the bulletin and you'll wish you hadn't."

Sunday's bulletin contained the following announcement:

PAPER SUPPLIES NEEDED

Members of the church who are physically and
financially able are asked to bring in periodic
donations of paper towels and toilet paper.
Please place them in the Lounge.
This will be an ongoing need.
Thank you for your help!

On Monday morning Trustee Chair Ken Johnson was sitting in Pastor John's office when he arrived.

"A lot of people are upset about that announcement in the bulletin, Pastor."

John's first thought: I've got to squelch this before Jean hears about it.

"Who are all these people, Ken?"

"Well," he said hesitatingly, a little taken back by the question, "my in-laws for two. And Mary's cousins. They're embarrassed by it. They think they give enough that the church can afford to buy toilet paper."

"You were at the finance committee meeting, Ken. You know the budget's awfully tight."

"Take it out of the Missions line item. If we've got enough money to give away, we ought to have enough money to buy toilet paper."

"The budget's been passed by the council, Ken, and approved by the charge conference. It's kinda set."

"Tell you what," Ken said with a hint of exasperation at John's lack of resourcefulness in his voice: "The Trustees will assume the responsibility; we'll buy the toilet paper and the paper towels and I'll personally get them distributed." Of course, the only place the Trustees could go to for money was the church treasury which had already been allocated for things other than donuts.

Pastor John was silent at lunch. "Why so quiet?" Jean asked.

"Oh, just thinking about Sunday's sermon," John replied.

When John walked into the office that afternoon, Mary, the church secretary, commented, "Ken was in a few moments ago; you just missed him."

"That's strange. He was here this morning too. What did he want?"

"He said something about checking out an air conditioner compressor. Said it needs leveling. He also mentioned the disgruntlement about the paper goods announcement. Lots of people are mad according to him. He said that the church has plenty of money and can certainly afford to buy toilet paper."

Pastor John went into his office, closed the door, sat down, promptly fell asleep, and began to dream.

* * * * *

He had no idea where he was. It was like he was surrounded by clouds. At times he had a fairly clear view ahead and then it would be obscured by an undulating whiteness. There was someone up in front speaking to him. The voice was a voice with authority in it, but still difficult to hear clearly. He sensed the whole scene had something to do with judgment. He was being judged. By whom? God?

He tried to move closer, but movement was an extreme challenge. His legs were bound together hips to knees He could only take baby steps and even those threatened to topple him over. His arms from his shoulders to his elbows seemed pinned to his sides, leaving only severely restricted forearm movements possible.

In seeming accommodation to John's physical limitations, the words spoken by the voice became louder and clearer.

"Tell us, please, what have you accomplished with your life? Have you fulfilled any of your dreams, your sense of purpose that you had when you were younger?"

Wow, what a question! Talk about striking at the heart of things.

"No," he responded. "I don't think I have. Some things have been very good, like marriage, children, times of friendship. These were goals, but I can't say I've fulfilled them as completely as I dreamed I would. There's always seemed to be some obstacle to getting to exactly where I wanted to be, where I felt I was going years ago."

"Maybe you would do better," the voice said, "if you would unfurl all that tissue paper that's wrapped around you."

* * * * *

John woke up with the final words of the voice echoing in his memory.

He got the message.

The voice was God.

And it revealed the plight of the human race. We humans are constantly allowing ourselves to be wrapped up in the mundane things of life and are thereby prevented from reaching out and seizing the brass ring of fulfillment and joy.

Ken and all his "lots of people" were permitting themselves to get wrapped up in the trivial issue of how toilet paper would be supplied. They got so wrapped up that they lost sight of the vision of church. Of course, toilet paper wasn't the only binding instrument. There were plenty of others, like donuts, like the color of carpet, like the music. In these ways the people of the church permitted themselves to be bound as strongly as Paul and Silas were bound by their chains and stocks in the Philippian jail. Only God could free Paul and Silas and through their unfettered worship God did just that.

John felt sorry for Ken and the others. Yet, he realized, he was as wrapped up in that toilet paper as the others were. In very short order it had become a defining issue for him. He felt sorry for himself. He prayed for forgiveness and for release from his bondage. Then he got up, opened the door, told Mary, "I'm leaving; I've got some loosening to do; see you tomorrow," and exited the office. He walked home, found Jean doing laundry in the basement, and asked, "Got time to go to Crow Creek Park and for a little Chinese afterwards?"

"Sure, she said. Just give me a few moments to get ready."

The park was in the center of the city, yet when one walked into the woods along the creek it put one in mind of a secluded wilderness. The sounds of urban life were muted if not completely extinguished. Walking along the trails, pausing on the creek bank and at the edge of the lagoon always gave John a sense of perspective he needed. Here, life was not a thing to be controlled but a thing to be experienced. Where better to worship God than in the midst of creation, John thought – in the woods and in the sanctuary, surrounded in each place by that which God has declared to be "good, very good"? He felt the chains loosening, the paper unraveling and falling at his feet. It was good. His mind turned toward the upcoming worship on Sunday when all God's grumbling and complaining people would gather together and love and hope would again gain the upper hand.

Jean too, he could tell, was experiencing a renewal of spirit, a freeing of soul. "Ready for that Chinese?" he inquired. "Yes – I am," she responded. "This has been good."

They drove to their favorite restaurant, The China Café, located in a small strip mall on one of the main thoroughfares of the city. Rose, whom John had always assumed was a member of the owning family, waited on them. She was preparing to leave for a trip home to Bejing where her mother and father resided. She was excited to be going despite the long flight with an infant. She told them a little about Bejing, how in many respects it was like here. It always amazed – and reassured – John how people are so very similar the world over. He observed it in Vietnam where he saw that despite all the war that was going on, people continued as much as they could to do the things people always do – plant and tend their crops, go to work, go to school, marry, have children, care for families. There is, he observed, a unity among us just waiting to be discovered in its fullness.

Finally, to conclude the evening, John and Jean paid a visit to the nearby bookstore. The baristas greeted them warmly and had their refreshments whipped out in no time. John sipped his café au lait and began a perusal of the *Times*. He read of horrors in Iraq, atrocities in Afghanistan, and cruelties at Guantanamo. How, he wondered, could people ever think that peace could be accomplished through war, that a better world could be created by violence? "Absurd!" scream the ages past. "Can't you learn?"

Yes, John pondered, we need to shed the things that bind us up, but we also must remove our blinders.

Chapter 3

A Gift from Ted

"Good morning, Mary. How are you today?"

"Hey, Pastor. I'm good."

"Anything happening?"

"Ted Fish called about a half an hour ago. Wants you to call him when you get a chance."

"Okay. Will do."

What, John wondered, did Ted want? As chair of the Staff-Parish Relations Committee it could be about a complaint someone had lodged with him. Given that it was Ted, it could concern any number of his personal grievances about the way John was fulfilling his role as pastor.

John liked Ted, even considered him a friend. He and Ted had had many good conversations and Ted could be very encouraging. He possessed lots of good ideas, but they often were couched negatively as if they were things that should've been done long ago rather than him having to bring them up now. Ted rarely seemed to recognize that many of his ideas were being implemented; John found that particularly frustrating.

John returned the call.

"Hi, Ted. Mary said you called."

"Yes, John. I have something I'd like to show you – and Jean if she's available. Would sometime this afternoon be okay for me to drop by the house?"

"Sure. How about around 1:30, right after lunch?"

"I'll be there."

"Bye."

Well, John pondered, I wonder just what he has to show us. Can't be too bad if he's including Jean. Say what you will about Ted, he's very respectful of one's family.

John threw himself into sermon preparation. He was in the early stages of a series on biblical figures, focusing on how each transformed the world for good or for evil. The coming Sunday's Bible character of emphasis was to be Noah.

What to say about Noah that is a lesson for today's people? Obedience is the usual piece about Noah – he obeyed God and built an ark even though everyone thought he was crazy. But I need to go deeper, John realized. Noah was obedient about the ark *why*? Because he was *prepared* to be obedient. Genesis 6: 9 relates that Noah "walked with

God." Whether one takes the whole story literally or not, the passage is important. For us to be prepared to seize the transformative opportunities God sends our way, we need to walk with God daily.

Pretty good stuff, John thought.

Then there's that rainbow. It's a symbol of God's grace. Yes, it is light refracted through raindrops – clearly scientifically explainable. But it's also one of God's ways of saying the beautiful order of things will continue if people don't mess everything up too much.

Ahh! The light bulb suddenly flashed on. That's what Ted was up to. He was going to quit the church, withdraw his membership. That's what he would give John today – his and Ellen's letter of withdrawal. They were leaving the church. Probably going to go to the Baptist church where Ted's cousin is a deacon.

He'd pushed Ted too far.[1] That argument over immigration in Bible study the other day had probably

---

[1] Not that there weren't people Pastor John would just as soon see leave the church. Ned Adams, for example. Ned was toxic. John would always painfully remember how Ned came up to him at the rear of the sanctuary one Sunday morning about two minutes before the processional and said, "You can tell that District Superintendent to take his ballots and stick them up his ass." Ned was hurting the church and himself; he needed to find a faith community more to his liking.

done it. Ted had declared that the government needed to take more decisive action against "illegals" since there was "simply no excuse for breaking the law." John had responded that Jesus and his family were likely illegal immigrants in Egypt according to our standards, and that we should think about that in relation to the "illegals" in our country. Would we run Jesus out? "Maybe," John went on, "that's exactly what we're doing when we deport all these people."

"The law is the law and it must be enforced," Ted reiterated. "Those people have to be taught that they can't keep illegally entering our country."

"Ted, if you were in the position many of them are – desperately poor and unable to provide for their families – I think you'd do exactly what they're doing. You'd cross the border any way you could if it meant a chance to make life better for your wife and children."

All this did not set well with Ted. When will I learn to keep my mouth shut? John asked himself.

Afternoon came and Jean and John awaited Ted's arrival. At precisely 1:30 he rang the doorbell.

"Come in, Ted."

"Hi, John, Jean. Sorry to intrude, but I have something I think you'll like. I don't know if you remember that afternoon rainstorm a few weeks ago, but at the tail end there was a terrific rainbow."

"As a matter of fact, I do," John replied. "I went out and looked at it. Most defined rainbow I've ever seen."

"Well," Ted continued, "my cousin who does a lot of photography and who lives across the highway over there took a picture of it and Ellen and I thought you'd like it. Here it is." Ted handed John a wrapped package.

As John tore off the wrapping, he saw that it was a beautifully framed picture. But when he clearly saw the photograph it took his breath away. It was a perfectly defined picture of the rainbow in all its glorious color arcing over the cross-topped steeple of the church.

"What a fantastic gift, Ted."

"You're welcome. Well, gotta go. Enjoy."

God's grace: It manifests itself in places you least expect it.

People: How sadly unaware we so often are of the depths of goodness within them.

Chapter 4

The Fall
or
Save Your Breath, They Won't Listen

It happened rather quickly.

According to the biblical account, man and woman were created, they were placed in a paradise, and they fell. Not a physical falling but a spiritual failing.

Not too long after entering into pastoral ministry Pastor John experienced a fall. His was definitely a physical fall, but upon examination a spiritual aspect could also be detected.

It happened on a Lakota Sioux reservation in South Dakota. The church was finally participating in a mission trip, something John had hoped for from the time he arrived. As it turned out, it was basically a youth trip although he hadn't planned it that way. The high school youth group quickly embraced the idea of the trip and that seemed to retard response from others; ultimately, the only adults on the journey were John and two youth group leaders.

A certain disgruntlement had settled into John's head and heart when he received news of the doings at an earlier youth group planning meeting which he had been unable to attend. His teenage daughter Ann reported it to him: "Sarah said she was scared of your driving because you tailgate too much, so Jim said he'd make sure you didn't drive the van at all."

Jim, the high school youth group leader, never mentioned this to John. Never talked to him about it. John stupidly didn't confront Jim with the impropriety of his making such a statement to the youth. Jim should've responded to Sarah with something like: I'll talk to Pastor John about your concern. Instead of addressing this issue with Jim, John let it fester, clearly the wrong thing to do spiritually. It was a don't-let-the-sun-go-down-on-your-anger sort of thing.

Despite the rockiness of his relationship with Jim, John thought he led a pretty impressive anointing service the evening before departure. He told the story reported in *Bury My Heart at Wounded Knee* of how Sioux wounded but not killed in a massacre by the cavalry were placed in the church where ironically the Christmas banner stretched across the chancel proclaimed: "Peace on earth, good will toward men."

"What peace? What good will?" John asked. "Given what had just happened to them, how could any Sioux who could read that banner accept Christianity? To him would not Jesus Christ be a bloodthirsty tyrant? Would he not be justified in saying, 'Curses on all Christians and on their god'?"

"It didn't get any better," John elaborated. The Sioux continued to be maltreated by the government and by the church. So don't expect the people where we're going to like you. Don't anticipate receiving thanks for your efforts. You are not trusted. Our efforts will be a small recompense for what their people suffered at the hands of our ancestors. We may say it's a victim mentality, but we cannot deny the wrong that was done."

Jim and Aaron, the other youth leader, diligently kept John from the front seats of the van during the entire trip to South Dakota. Not that John necessarily wanted to drive, but he thought their conduct was arrogant as well as improper (even un-Christian, perhaps). But at that point he couldn't find any way to appropriately address the situation. The anger, particularly toward Jim, continued to build.

John and some of the youth were assigned to work on a new house being constructed outside the town of Mission, just off the reservation proper John was told. Included in John's squad was Jerry, a sixteen or seventeen-year-old who was not a member of the church's youth group. He was the brother of Larry who had ties to the group through his girlfriend. Jerry attracted trouble. He had at times left home and his parents seemed to have pretty much given up on him. Not too much later John would visit him in jail.

Yes, Jerry attracted trouble, but Jerry and his brother Larry together were trouble. Their relationship was dangerously volatile. One evening Pastor John was in the bathroom brushing his teeth and doing some preliminary getting-ready-for-bed things when Jerry burst into the room, blood streaming from his nose.

"He punched me."

"Who punched you?"

"Larry, my so-called brother, that's who!"

At that moment Larry came running down the hall, hands raised and clenched into fists. John grabbed the bathroom door and attempted to slam it closed, but before he could get the job done, Larry was pushing back and spewing forth a stream of profanities. John finally got the door closed, latched, and locked. Larry then resorted to pounding on the door in rhythm with his cursing. It was almost rap-like.

"What's all this about?" John demanded as Jerry held his bloody nose over the sink and splashed water on it from his cupped hands.

"I just told him that he was getting a little too lovey-dovey with Suzie and he off and popped me in the nose."

"I can't believe you said that to him, Jerry. You guys were warned before we came to keep your opinions to yourselves. For this one week you are expected to let the irritants, the insults, the obnoxiousness of others roll off your back. You failed in that. I believe we'll have to consider calling your folks and asking them to come get you."

"But he's the one who hit me."

"And you're the one who opened your big mouth, Jerry. Besides, Larry should be sent home too."

By this time Larry had cooled and left the doorway. Jerry got the bleeding stopped and then joined the rest of the group, Larry included, without further incident. An uneasy peace reigned.

John, Jim, and Aaron gathered outside the house and after discussion agreed that sending the boys home wasn't practicable. Their parents would probably refuse to come and get them. Jim was designated to talk with Larry and John was to continue his dialogue with Jerry. Fortunately, there were no more major conflicts.

The workers at the house were charged primarily with the tasks of applying the pressboard siding and the steel roofing. It was in the roofing part that John almost – but not quite – had his fall.

Scaffolding had been erected on the north side of the house for the purpose of putting on the siding. This particular day, the roofing people were also using it to facilitate hauling sheets of roofing onto the top of the house. John, who had been working on the siding, aided the roofing crew in wrangling a few pieces of steel. As he prepared to get off the roof, he decided he'd just jump onto the scaffolding rather than using the ladder that ran down to the planking. Somehow Jerry – who was quite a distance away on the roof – perceived what John was about to do. He started yelling: "John! Stop! Don't jump!"

John, intent on doing the most macho thing he could, was inclined to ignore Jerry. He didn't want to listen to anyone. Yet Jerry's calls caused him to pause, and upon pausing he saw the problem. The planks upon which John was going to jump were extended beyond the scaffolding; if he jumped on them they would not support him, but would tip and he would crash to the ground and onto all the debris that lay upon it. He could easily have been killed. John was indebted to Jerry for his life.

Later Pastor John ended up working on the roof again. His job was to follow along the edge of the roof on a ladder and insert a foam insect barrier as each sheet of roofing was laid down by the workers above. Each successive piece became more difficult because each sheet protruded farther over the edge.

"Hey, I don't think you're laying this roofing straight," John called to the others.

"It's good," one of them replied.

"No it's not. They're not square. By the time we get to the end we'll be hanging over six inches or more."

"No worry. We measured it all out before we started."

John's fall came on Friday, the last full day of the trip. The squad arrived at the house early that morning and began the process of tearing off the plywood they had nailed across the windows and doors Thursday evening to discourage theft of the wiring and plumbing. Given the slope of the ground, stepladders were needed to reach the top of the window frames in order to pull the nails there. John was on a ladder at one end of a picture window and one of the youth from another church was on a ladder at the other end. The kid was goofing off and in the process knocked his ladder into John's. John saw what was coming and madly started climbing down, but too late. The other ladder crashed into his and he and his ladder went tumbling backwards down the slope. He hit hard on his left side, miraculously missing the tools, lumber, nails, and other assorted items scattered on the ground.

The ambulance seemed to take forever to get there. With assistance John had managed to make it to the cab of a nearby truck where he could sit in some comfort. His shoulder had issues; he couldn't move his arm without a lot of pain. Something, he feared, was broken.

As John rode to the hospital, the paramedic expressed how good he thought it was that the church groups were there. "This place is full of evil," he said, "In my work I see it all the time. Only through people bringing in the word of God and the Spirit of Jesus will things ever change. Only Christ can exorcise the demons that are legion here."

The paramedic's words brought back to John's recollection an earlier experience in the area. It had been only a year previously when John and his family went to the Black Hills and Mount Rushmore for a vacation trip. As they drove through the Pine Ridge reservation, John had begun to feel uncomfortable. A feeling of unease came over him, as if there were some intangible threat surrounding him. It was a sense of the presence of evil. It didn't lift until they drove beyond the boundaries of the reservation, but even then, it didn't fully dissipate. It persisted through the night and even into the next day. John understood that the paramedic was talking about the same sort of experience.

When John got to the hospital, a very painful x-ray procedure revealed that he had broken the ball joint in his shoulder. Surgery would not be helpful. They gave him a sling and doped him up on morphine. He was ravenously hungry, so a kind nurse brought him some lunch. As he sat there on the emergency room cot eating his lunch, he heard the communications radio squawking in the next room. Another casualty had occurred at the worksite. One of the men from another church had fallen off the roof and been seriously injured – seemingly much more seriously than John. He and some others had been taking off the sheets of roofing because they weren't square! The men had been hurrying because the week was coming to an end and in their haste one of them had tumbled over the edge. If only they had listened to John a day or two earlier.

Manifestations of evil? Does evil somehow have the power to drive goodness away? As a result of the two incidents, work was halted and the mission teams left a day earlier than scheduled. Did they run too soon? Should they have stayed to somehow confront the spiritual forces of darkness more completely?

When John got back to the church in Illinois, the word was, of course, already there. The prayer chain had been activated shortly following his injury. The word, though, wasn't quite accurate. The story that came down was "Pastor John fell off a ladder." For a while John kept trying to set people straight because "falling" seemed to imply a clumsiness on his part. "No," he said, "I didn't *fall off* the ladder; my ladder was *pushed over* with me on it." But no one seemed interested in listening. They continued to talk about Pastor John's "fall."

It's so true. We people don't listen very well. We hear what we want to hear. Sometimes we miss out on very important truths when we do that. Sometimes it doesn't matter. John decided the precise truth about whether he fell or was accidentally pushed didn't matter much, and he stopped correcting people. But the truth about evil is another matter entirely. The truth there is important. Was evil resident in Mission, South Dakota, as the paramedic said? Was the outbreak between Jerry and Larry a symptom of that presence? Did John perhaps transport a measure of evil to South Dakota through his anger toward Jim and Aaron?

Chapter 5

Raccoons, Darkness, and the Cross

Saturday night.

He was on the pulpit side of the chancel getting things ready for Sunday morning when the lights went out. Suddenly. No flickering. No on and off as they often did when there was a storm. One moment they were on and the next moment they were out.

No sound either. No sound of a transformer blowing out from age, excess demand, or squirrel.

The darkness was absolute. The small stained glass windows admitted no light from the outside. Thus, reasoned Pastor John, the outage must be spread farther than the church building or some rays from the parking lot or road lighting would surely filter through.

He moved slowly, shuffling his feet, advancing in the direction he thought the chancel steps lay. It seemed to be taking longer than it should. Just as he stumbled onto the lectern he was blinded by the light – the intense beam of a powerful flashlight. It was Jean who'd come over from the darkened parsonage and rescued him out of his own darkness.

"Thank you!" John exclaimed. "I was totally turned in the wrong direction. It's unbelievably dark in here. Any idea how widespread this is?"

"No. I haven't looked beyond here."

"So let's go out front and see if there are any lights on across the road."

John and Jean made their way through the church kitchen to the exit. As John pushed the door open he heard a soft thud and felt some resistance to the door's opening. When Jean came up behind him the flashlight illuminated the obstacle – a raccoon. The door had pushed it a little way down the walk, but it didn't seem particularly inclined to move any further. Then they saw two or three others clustered at the foot of the dumpster.

"Good grief," John said. "I've never seen raccoons around here like this. In all the years we've been here I've only once encountered a raccoon at the dumpster. Now all of a sudden there are four."

"That's not all," Jean replied. She shined the beam of the flashlight up the church drive toward the main doors and there were several more raccoons staring at them.

"Wow! They're really behaving strangely." As soon as John said this, the raccoons, seemingly on cue, began to chatter among themselves.

"What a strange night," Jean said, expanding on John's earlier comment. It was then that they saw all the flashing red lights at the curve in the road about a quarter or half mile north. They could make out several police cars, an ambulance, and a fire truck.

"Where did they come from?" John wondered aloud. "I didn't hear any sirens, did you?"

"No," Jean replied.

"A strange night."

They procured a couple of lawn chairs from the parsonage garage and sat in the front yard for it was a warm night and the breeze was cooling to the skin. Jean knitted which she could do without seeing and John reviewed his Sunday sermon with the aid of a flashlight. John also paused periodically to silently voice a prayer for whoever needed assistance up the road and for those workers providing that assistance.

Fifteen minutes, half-an-hour, an hour. The emergency vehicles were still there.

"Not a good omen," John said. "They are in no hurry to get anyone to the hospital."

After about an hour-and-a-half, John turned off the flashlight, stood up, and suggested, "I think it's time to get some sleep if we can. Hopefully the power and the air conditioning will come back on pretty soon; otherwise we're going to have a pretty warm night."

John didn't find out what had happened until Donna came early Sunday morning to make the coffee and set up the snacks. "A young man was killed out here on the road last night," she announced.

"Omigosh! What happened?"

"Well, I don't know for sure, but what I've heard is that he was doing about a hundred. When he went into the S-curve, the car shot right off the road. It went behind the guard rail on the other side of the road and became airborne. He flew over that little creek down there and snapped off a utility pole. They say he was killed instantly."

"Wow!" John exclaimed. "What a tragedy. How old was he?"

"Nineteen or twenty, twenty-one. Somewhere in there."

"What a waste. Alcohol or drugs involved?"

"No one knew. Would assume so, though, given how it happened. He could've just fallen asleep, but I wouldn't think a person would fall asleep while driving a hundred miles an hour."

John thought about the previous night. At the very moment the light in the sanctuary went out, a life was extinguished. Just like that. One second the room was filled with light and beauty, the next second it was dark. One second the young man was alive, the next second he was dead. As the apostle James observed, "What is your life? You are a mist that appears for a little while and then vanishes."

It was much the same with Terry Jones. A key leader in the church. In choir. Treasurer. Liturgist. A voice of experience, reason, and faith. What a blessing he and his wife Fay were from almost the moment Pastor John and Jean arrived. Terry had a heart condition. He'd had some surgery, but pulled through and had done fine for quite some time. Then there was a light snowfall – maybe an inch – and Terry fatefully decided he could shovel such a small amount. He was wrong and his error cost him his life. Fay had gone to work that morning leaving a reasonably vibrant husband at home; when she returned that afternoon, he wasn't there. She could tell something had happened because the furniture was out of place. The message was on the answering machine: "Your husband is at the hospital; come as soon as you get this message." On Valentine's Day morning, Fay had had a sweetheart; by Valentine's Day evening, she was alone.

John was not called upon to do the young man's funeral. Maybe he had some church affiliation although it seemed like so very few young people did any more. John went on with the usual church business the following week. The raccoons were settled down and he didn't see any the entire week. On Thursday he and Jean put a new message on the church sign out by the road. It was related to the upcoming Sunday's message, and it read: "The cross – a sign of hope."

On Monday morning this message was on the church voice mail:

> Hello. My name is Marjorie Somerville and I live in the Deer Prairie housing development next to the

church. I want you to know that I appreciate the messages that have been out on your church sign. They have been very inspiring and I feel bad I haven't called to thank you for them. However, the present piece about the cross is maybe not the best, given the circumstances. I don't know if you're aware, but a young man was killed less than a mile from your church. My son and others who were his friends have placed a cross out at the site of the accident, and they are upset about the words on the sign. They certainly don't see the cross as a sign of hope, but of death. Maybe you want to reconsider what's out there.

Pastor John's anger flared up immediately. No way do I want to reconsider the message, John thought. That's exactly the message I intended – the cross, despite the human evil it represents, is the ultimate expression of hope because Jesus didn't stay dead; Jesus defeated not only the instrument of death, but death itself. That gives us hope.

John considered calling Ms. Somerville and attempting to explain all this to her. But he decided instead to change the sign. So he gathered up some more letters, went out and opened up the sign, and placed these words upon it: "The cross – a sign of the hope of resurrection and life eternal." What, he thought, could be better news?

Marjorie didn't call again. He hoped she and her son saw and understood. He hoped he was right.

Chapter 6

Angels in the Belfry

He couldn't precisely identify when he began hearing the voices.

It was early on in his tenure at the church – of that he was sure. And it was on a Saturday night in the sanctuary. As usual, he was there about ten o'clock practicing delivery of Sunday's sermon, trying to memorize the substance and some of the precise phrasing. He paused and then he heard it, the faint sound of voices coming from above.

He cocked his right ear to try to better hear. The words were indistinguishable but they sounded like conversation. He went into the sacristy and the loudness increased, but not enough to understand or to locate the origin. Then it began to resemble singing. The tune was familiar, but again not enough volume to put a name to it. Someone more astute at recognizing songs could maybe name it, but Pastor John could not.

Well, he thought, no demons could enter into this holy place, so it must be angels. The voices of angels. In that he took comfort, encouragement, and joy. "For he will command his angels concerning you to guard you in all your ways," the Bible says. In fulfillment of the scripture, God had dispatched angels to this new place in which he found himself. What better place could there be to be? That was the attitude he adopted toward the voices heard in the sanctuary.

But the angels didn't stay at the sanctuary. He encountered them everywhere, and upon reflection he recognized that they had been with him at other places and times as well:

1.

There was Lori, a fellow pastor at the cooperative. At an early staff meeting where a possible retreat was being discussed, John had asked, "Who have you had as retreat leaders previously?"

"Most recently," Lori replied, "we had John McFarland. He's a retired pastor living in Sterling or one of those towns along I-88. Did a phenomenal job inspiring us."

"Wow!" John exclaimed. "John McFarland and I grew up in the same town in southern Indiana. He was the older brother to one of my very best friends in grade school and junior high. I got the opportunity to hear him at a conference in Washington, Illinois, and I agree that he is outstanding. Wish I had been here to participate in your retreat with him."

Following the meeting and for the next day or two John experienced what he dubbed a "nostalgic sadness," brought on by all the memories that came flooding back through the reminder of his home town and the people he had known there and likely would never see again.

Later that week Lori came by his office. She was carrying a book.

"I brought this by for you. I thought you might enjoy it." She handed him the book. It was a signed copy of *The Strange Calling* by Pastor McFarland. Pastor John flipped to the first page of the first chapter and read this: "It was the annual Memorial Day softball game, between the men and the boys of the Forsythe Methodist Church." John didn't attend the Forsythe Church when he was a boy, but he'd been to the little country house of worship with his friend Jim. As he read, it was like he was there once again.

"Gee thanks, Lori. I'll get it back to you as soon as I get it read."

"No, keep it. It's a gift."

At that point Lori was one of God's angels, sent to bring a measure of solace and comfort and to turn the nostalgic sadness into joy.

2.

Then there was Terry Jones, officially lay leader and church treasurer, unofficially the go-to man for most anything that needed to be done in the church. John had gotten himself worked up over an upcoming church council meeting. He tried to prepare to the ultimate degree. A couple of hours before the meeting he came out of the pastor's study into the church office. Terry was there paying bills and John mentioned the meeting to him. "If they'll only cooperate and follow the agenda, we'll be okay," he said.

Terry looked at him in that unique way he had and asked what he obviously believed was a rhetorical inquiry: "You don't really think you are in charge, do you?"

Terry was another angel, sent this time to free John from the burden of self-importance and to give him a good laugh. And laugh is exactly what he did. He looked at Terry, saw the caring in his face, and laughed like he hadn't laughed for a very long time. It was okay, for the laughter was directed at himself.

3.

Charlotte. She was named after her father Charlie. She wasn't supposed to be alive. She was born in the cold winter of Kansas. Stillborn, they said. They laid her little body on a shelf in the unheated mudroom. The other children, their curiosity aroused, played with dead Charlotte on her shelf. Suddenly all the movement wasn't induced by them. Charlotte was beginning to animate her arms and legs. The children, maybe not fully understanding death but certainly recognizing life, went shrieking into the parlor where the adults were gathered, "She's alive! She's alive!"

Charlotte was in her seventies when Pastor John met her. She was a member of his first congregation. Charlotte was a tall woman, considerably taller than John, and in that way somewhat intimidating to him. But when he saw her smile after service on that first Sunday, he knew they were going to become good friends. And they did.

During this time, John's mother began experiencing a rapid decline in her mental health. In a futile attempt to provide more care, John and Jean purchased the house next to the church from a relocating church member and made it a home for John's mom. Things did not go well. Ruth had lost the ability to relate to other people, even members of her own family. Her seeming lack of caring frustrated John beyond reason and caused him to lash out at her, sometimes even cruelly. He knew that there was no way that his relationship with his mother would be restored. He knew that she had little control over her behavior. Yet he fruitlessly kept trying to connect with her as if nothing had changed.

One beautiful summer day John was walking to the church when he encountered Charlotte walking toward him. They both stopped and talked a while. The conversation eventually turned to Ruth.

"Caroline's telling everyone your mother says she hates you because you're so mean to her." Caroline was

Ruth's neighbor. "I know what your mom's saying isn't true, but I didn't want you to hear it from someone who might be nasty about it."

"Thanks," John replied.

"Just don't let it get you down, John. There's only so much you can do, and you're doing it."

Charlotte on that day was truly an angel to John, as she would be again on other days yet to come.

4.

September 11, 2001 – another beautiful late-summer day in west central Illinois. Pastor John had an early appointment for his physical therapy (necessitated by the South Dakota incident). Even though he was not a "morning person," he truly enjoyed the twenty-minute drive to Galesburg. The bright yellow sunlight on the changing trees and on the crisp corn and soybean fields reminded him powerfully of God's abundant provision and grace. All seemed right with the world.

In the midst of walking his hand up and down the wall and working the pulleys, John heard the voice of a new arrival. It was saying something about a plane crashing into the World Trade Center in New York. John assumed for some unknown reason that it was a light plane that had become disoriented somehow. An accident. The radio station music was playing through the ceiling speakers without interruption so the incident couldn't have been too serious. No further information came to John's attention during the next half hour or so as he finished up his therapy and paid his bill.

The first thing John did when he got into his car was to tune the radio to the local NPR station; he heard only classical music. But he hadn't driven very far before the symphony was interrupted and the announcer began giving more detail about what was happening in New York City and also in Washington, D.C.: At 7:48 a.m. Central Time, American Airlines Flight 11 had crashed into Tower 1; at 8:03 United Flight 175 had impacted Tower 2; and at 8:41 American Airlines Flight 77 had struck the Pentagon. Before the sinking feeling in his stomach had even begun to abate, the radio announced that Tower 2 had totally collapsed.

He reached the village of New Windsor and stopped at the Glenns where he was picking up some items for church. Lois Glenn came out the door of her house as he pulled into the gravel turnout alongside the highway, her face showing that she was aware of what was going on in the eastern part of the country. They exchanged a hug, Lois gave him the items he had come for, they joined hands, and they prayed. Then John got back into his car and headed toward the Rock Island hospital where he planned to visit Linda who was there because of some developing difficulties in her pregnancy.

As John drove on, hearing about the crash of United Flight 93 in a Pennsylvania field, the collapse of Tower 1, and the fact that almost no one was showing up in the New York hospitals because there were no survivors (blood donations were not needed), he thought about the contrasts in his day: Death in New York, Washington, and Pennsylvania; a struggle for new life in Rock Island, Illinois. Prayers for the dead; prayers for the hope of life.

The more he pondered what was happening, the greater the horror seemed. What would cause people to commit such atrocious acts where thousands of innocents were killed? He thought of all the children who would never again see the mothers and fathers who left them that morning to go to work, or who were intent on flying home to be with them. He thought of the wives and husbands who had held each other in bed that morning for the last time. What brought the world to this state? He knew it wasn't isolated fault. It wasn't just Middle-Eastern terrorists. It was all of us – American, Arab, Palestinian, Christian, Jew, Muslim. Violence begets violence – a scriptural truth. He himself had participated in the never-ending cycle when he mindlessly killed in Southeast Asia. Is there any hope for any of us? he thought. If so, where is it?

"How you doing?" John asked Linda as he walked over to the bedside after greeting her husband Teddy.

"Great compared to those poor people in New York, Washington, and Pennsylvania. Who would do such terrible things?"

"All of us. Any one of us. It's the Genesis story. Each of us is capable of doing awful things and it's only through a healthy relationship with God that we can hedge the evil that seeks to control us. Sorry about the sermon, but I've been thinking it all the way up here and your question prompted the delivery."

"That's okay. I know you're right, but I really want someone to blame for this and I need for whoever it is to be a much worse person than I am."

"Yeah, you're not alone in that," John responded. "Anyhow, what's going on with you, Linda? Exactly why are you here?"

"The baby wants to come out but it's way too early. It needs at least another four weeks to be viable. So the doctor wants me on bed-rest until that time passes."

"Wow! That's going to be a challenge I would think. Do you have to stay here in the hospital for all that time?"

"They want me to stay a couple more days for observation. Then, if things look reasonably stable, I can go home if I promise to stay in bed."

"Well," John offered, "at least you should be able to catch up on your reading. How about you, Teddy, are you ready to take over the housekeeping chores as well as going to work?"

"You bet!" Teddy answered. "Linda's mom Pat and Grandma Charlotte will help out during the day when I can't be there. We'll get the job done."

"I'm confident you will," John said. If anyone can, you can, with God's help. Speaking of God's help, let's pray."

The call from Pat came on Pastor John's Sabbath – his personal day off. He was relaxing in the bookstore coffee shop with Jean when his cell rang. "They're taking Linda to the operating room. Something's gone wrong. It's not good."

"Jean will call the prayer chain and I'll be right there."

On the drive to the hospital John computed how long it had been since Linda started the bed-rest regimen. Three weeks. Not as much as they had wanted. "Lord," he prayed, "bless Linda and that baby. Make them both whole and healthy so that they might be witnesses to your goodness, so they might share your love with the world."

As he entered the obstetrics floor of the hospital and headed toward the surgical area, John glanced down the hallway to his immediate left and saw Linda's family gathered in front of the nursery viewing window. He knew then that all was well. He walked down the hall toward them delighting in the smiles he saw on their faces and thanking God for the blessing. When he got there the nurse was just bringing little Arial to the window.

There was his angel – his angel of hope. Arial was the answer, he realized, to his question of hope. Hope is in the abiding presence of God and in the promise of the newborn child. "Into the darkness a light has come . . . and a little child shall lead them." The year 2001 had been redeemed for Pastor John in the sight of the struggling life before him.

* * * * *

It was about ten o'clock on a clear, cold night in Advent. The committee meetings were over and the church emptied of people. John was making his rounds adjusting thermostats, picking up trash, gathering up coffee cups, flushing toilets, turning off lights. He had stepped outside to switch off the lighted nativity scene on the front yard when he heard the music more distinctly than ever before. It was Charles Wesley's classic carol, *Hark! the Herald Angels Sing*, emanating from the steeple. The song finished and the announcer's voice came on: "This is WKQC bringing you the best of the music of Christmas . . ."

The voices John had been hearing all that time were the voices of a radio station! He knew of no radio in the steeple. And the voices weren't always there. Was it not perhaps possible that the radio station was an instrument of the angels, a means of God's grace? Pastor John liked to think so.

Chapter 7

War Prayer

Late September, 2001, Kansas City, Missouri.

They were at a Promise Keepers gathering of tens of thousands of men in Kansas City's enormous Kemper Arena. Eight of them had made the six-hour trip in Sage Riverton's van. Jim and Aaron were among the eight so, of course, they did all the driving. Although the convention was being held in the shadow of September 11, the overall theme was the honor due pastors.

Pastor John had attended a number of Promise Keeper events. While he didn't always relate to some of the conservative theology that was promulgated, he did embrace the PK assertion that American men had generally abandoned their spiritual responsibilities, especially to their families. He'd seen it with his church's annual reports showing the memberships becoming increasingly female. He'd seen it as women had to step up to take more and more leadership roles in the church because of the dearth of men to fill them. There was, in John's view, a rapidly growing gender imbalance which was not good for the church and the fulfillment of its mission to transform the world. So he supported Promise Keepers because he had witnessed how it encouraged men to become disciples and fulfill their responsibilities to their families, their places of employment, their communities, and their churches. The families of PK men seemed to thrive in the church and that, John thought, had to be good.

After Friday evening's session, they were stuck in the parking lot for a very long time as departing cars slowly made their way onto the street. They talked some about the evening's presentations, but the conversation soon drifted to the subject of war. When would the American strikes in retaliation for September 11 begin? At some point Pastor John queried of the group: "Actually, shouldn't we pray that there will be no war, no military retaliation, and that a diplomatic, peaceful approach will be found?"

Rod responded, "We can pray it but it ain't going to happen that way."

"Why not? Why can't prayer change the outcome?"

"I dunno. I just can't see it happening."

"I understand where you're coming from, Rod. Often it does seem terrible things happen in spite of our prayers. Yet I have faith in the power of prayer. I've experienced things happening that I think were the result of prayer. When I was a lawyer, I witnessed litigation settled in a way that I believe never would've happened absent the intervention of God through prayer. I'm here as a pastor of your church because of prayer. Remember a number of years back when we were ready to invade Haiti?"

"Yeah."

"I felt the invasion got cancelled because of my prayers. For days I'd been praying every morning for a non-military resolution, and then it came about just as I had prayed."

"Do you still think your prayer prevented the war?" Aaron interjected.

"Yes. Mine and all the like prayers uttered by an untold number of other people. Jesus said, 'Ask and you shall receive.' I can't pretend to know exactly how it works, but I believe we are called to take Jesus up on the offer in a spirit of positive expectation."

"But don't you think the United States needs to retaliate for the atrocity that's been inflicted on it with the complicity of the Afghanistan government?" Aaron continued.

"Jesus never said to retaliate against anyone. He told us to love our enemies, not to take revenge on them. In war there's no room for love; war precludes love. Love can't come out of the end of a gun. Paul said we are to provide and care for our enemies, not kill them. When we go to war, we're not on Jesus' side.

"I wonder why we are always so seemingly eager to take up arms," John continued. "It's like we can't remember how awful it is. We've seen the horrors of the likes of Gettysburg, the death-trap trenches, the poison gas, the Blitz, Guadalcanal, the Bulge, Dresden, Hiroshima, Pork Chop Hill, Hamburger Hill, My Lai – the list can go on and on. Yet we rush in. Why does there always seem to be so many more voices for war than for peacemaking?

"Whenever I think of war, I think of my friend Gordon. We met in a theater of war. Gordon was my age, a young college graduate hailing from Boston, a red-haired Irish boy. He had a girlfriend and a life planned back in Massachusetts, but the nation's thirst for blood dispatched him to the jungles of Vietnam.

"Gordon and I did the same job in Fire Direction Control. We worked out of the FDC bunker and slept in another bunker, thirty or so feet away. I use the term "bunker" loosely when I refer to our sleeping quarters. It consisted of some stacked ammo boxes topped with culvert and then a couple of layers of sandbags filled with dirt.

"It was night. Around midnight. I woke up, slipped on my fatigues, and crawled out of the bunker into the danger zone – the open area I had to cross to get to the control center. It was safe on this night, though; there was no incoming.

"I greeted Gordon. He got up and I took his chair. He left.

"The explosion rattled the bunker a little, but that was it. It did a lot more to Gordon. It destroyed his body. The open area wasn't safe for him. Our own mortar team had miscalculated and brought their rounds down on our own camp. Gordon was killed by the "friendly fire" of war.

"That's what war is — the waste of life. Why can't we human beings seem to remember that for any length of time?"

* * * * *

When the bombs fell and the war started, Pastor John was at another retreat — a Walk to Emmaus weekend. It was Sunday, his daughter Ann's sixteenth birthday, and in the midst of these joys the nation was marching into the killing fields of Afghanistan.

At dinner the night before John had sat next to Lisa, one of the musicians on the weekend. He admired her music and her testimony about how God was working in her life, but he was disturbed by a comment she made at dinner: "We are so fortunate George Bush was elected president last year," she said. "I hate to think what it would be like if Al Gore were in charge."

What, John wondered, would Al Gore do under the circumstances that would be so terrible? Maybe he would find an alternative to war. Maybe he would find a way to address the situation without killing a bunch more people. Would that be so awful? Maybe he would end up in a war just like George Bush. He didn't vocalize his thoughts to

Lisa for he didn't wish to engage in the political conversation that likely would ensue. He simply prayed that it would all soon be over.

Once the war got going it apparently became evident to many in the upper echelons of the power structure that one war was not enough. So they invaded Iraq on false pretenses. To Pastor John it was the 1964 Gulf of Tonkin scam all over again. Before the planned invasion actually took place, he wrote and preached about it, pointing out that the action could not in any way be squared with the just war doctrine, if indeed any war could be deemed just. Reluctant as he was to attribute such callousness and jadedness to the nation's leaders, he ultimately had to admit that the war was about oil.

* * * * *

The years passed. The wars continued.

Afghanistan had seemingly devolved into a half-hearted attempt at revenge. Iraq had moved to center stage. That's where the real show was, where American deaths alone were moving into the thousands. The national economy had, in a perverse way, become increasingly dependent on the wars. The wars were accomplishing their objective of making the rich richer while also providing employment for the underclass as cannon fodder. The draining of the national treasure, however, seemed to be conveniently ignored by the makers of policy.

Pastor John was frustrated. How to speak of this to those who filled the pews and were content – nay, happy – with the possibility of receiving some crumbs of imperialism, some drippings of petro wealth? Maybe a job. Maybe a steady supply of unreasonably cheap gasoline. Certainly more dead boys and girls to provide fuel for the national pyre of patriotism.

Jesus said, "Where your treasure is, there will be your heart also." In John's eyes, too many people treasured flag-waving and drive-through fast food, with their hearts pledged to whatever would provide the greatest amount of cheap stuff to fill their rented storage units. Sometimes, Pastor John thought, religious people seemed to be the most afflicted with this American disease. Couldn't they see that Jesus would never condone this way of life?

And the wars plodded on.

"I think you're going into depression," Jean said to John one morning.

John continued looking into the bathroom mirror, contemplated Jean's assertion for a moment, and then replied, "Maybe. There's just so much bad thinking going on, and Christians seem to be championing a lot of it. How is any of this living the way of Jesus? And where is God in all this?"

"John, you can't change everything that's wrong with the world. You have to focus on the specific things you can do."

"Sometimes I think the very best thing we all could do is to stop doing so much. We are always thinking we've got to do something and it's all this activity that causes so much trouble."

"You may have a point there."

"I think back to when I was a kid. I was a lazy kid. In some ways I've tried to make up for that my whole life. And I don't know if much good has come out of the effort.

"In the summers as a kid I loved to ride my bike down to the town library which was located in the upstairs of the city hall/police department building. It was right across the tracks from the train depot and across the street from the American Legion. The barrels of the Legion's cannons were pointed directly at the library as though the real threat to humanity came from all those books.

"Anyway, I'd ride down there on those summer afternoons, park my bike, climb the oil-soaked stairs, and enter my refuge from the world and from the danger of being put to work. Old (I thought she was real old) Mrs. Miller would greet me with as much warmth as a librarian could muster in those days. On a great day she'd say, 'We just got a new Hardy Boys book in. It's on the shelf back there.' I'd hurry to the rear of the library, pull out the new volume, sit down at the table, and read for the rest of the afternoon.

"Other days I'd run down to our neighbor's pond across the street and cast off in the old rowboat they had there. I'd lie in the bottom of the boat just looking up at the tops of the trees and the birds flying across the bright blue of the sky. Multi-colored dragonflies would alight on the gunwales, and my imagination would soar.

"I know I'm romanticizing the past, but my point is there's a power in a certain amount of idleness. And some activities are more sublime than others. I wish everyone would spend more time in the libraries and floating on the ponds, or in some peaceful equivalents that appeal to each individual. Simply put, we need to cultivate good forms of laziness."

"There you have it," said Jean. "You need to encourage not only observation of the Sabbath, but a Sabbath view of life."

Jane and John's conversation was interrupted by the ringing of John's phone.

"Hi, pastor. This is Art. Hey, I'm going to the picketing down at the mall on Saturday morning. Want to come along?"

John hesitated, thinking about the possible ramifications. Would he catch a lot of flak if seen by someone in the congregation? Should he take such a public position? He didn't think long, quickly realizing that if he truly believed all the things he'd said about the war, he had to do it.

"Sure, Art. Thanks for asking. What time do they start?"

"Ten o'clock, when a lot of the mall stores open."

"See ya there."

"Okay."

After he hung up the phone, he relayed the details of the conversation to Jean. She asked, "What do you see this picketing accomplishing?"

"Well, I've sensed that the results in the last election have been viewed by the presidential administration as an endorsement by the American people of the war in Iraq. And the ordinary citizen is, I think, being sucked in by that thinking. It is important that people are aware that there is opposition, that there is a way of thinking about this thing other than the one advanced by those in power in Washington. The demonstration is about keeping the issue out in front of people, of making sure they don't forget that there is a war going on and that lots of other people are dying and suffering in many ways because of it. It's one way of doing that."

"Makes sense. Did you remember that Laura is coming in on Friday evening?"

"Oops! No, I didn't, but it's only going to take a couple of hours of my time. And maybe she'll want to come along."

When Saturday came, John's daughter Laura was happy to participate. She, like her dad, thought it important to keep the war issue out in front of people so that it wouldn't sink into a war of complacency that could go on for a very long time indeed.

The picketing took place at the busiest intersection in the city. John found the reactions of those passing by to be very revealing about the nature of war in the United States. Unsurprisingly, there were a number of negative responses – fists shaken at them, fingers extended toward them, foul language shouted in their direction. It was impossible to know how a passing car's occupants would react, except for one consistent thing – if the occupants of the car were other-than-white, they would almost always indicate their support of the picketers, by a honk and a thumbs-up or by vocal cheers of encouragement. They, John understood, were likely members of the socio-economic class who most often had to bear the trauma of war. They were experiencing the reality of war first-hand.

The picketing on Saturdays helped John shake off his depression. As the country headed into another presidential election cycle, strong voices were being raised in opposition to the Iraq adventure. There was a little more hope in the air that what John called "the long national nightmare" would end and that he would soon wake up to a day when he once again could hold his head up as an American. John was more convinced than ever of the need to pray, to pray boldly and expectantly for no more war, and to help create spaces where hope can seep in.

Chapter 8

I'm Just Passing Through

Georgia had done an amazing job with the Sunday School. She had managed to establish five children and youth classes in the little church. As she put it, she had "beaten the bushes" finding kids to bring to Sunday School. When she started, her daughter was three and a primary motivator for her activity; when Pastor John arrived, the daughter was thirteen.

Effective as she was, Georgia didn't seem to have close relationships in the church. While there was respect for her work – the teachers praised her diligence and organizational skills – there was also a certain amount of fear of her. She was brusque. She was volatile – cordial, even warm, one day and combative the next day.

John's first encounter with the difficulty of Georgia occurred in connection with the Christmas program. It was at the end of October or first of November. A Sunday afternoon. Pat phoned him at home and told him of a conflict that had occurred that morning.

"I was just trying to help out when she let me have it with both barrels," Pat told him.

"How did it all get started?" John asked.

"Last Sunday I was in the copier room and Georgia was talking to one of the teachers about all the work she had facing her in regard to the Christmas program. She said she just didn't know how she was going to get it all done."

"Uh huh."

"So I offered to help. I said I'd be happy to do whatever she needed – work on scripts, make sets, assist at rehearsals."

"What did she say?"

"She said, 'Great, I could really use the help.'"

"So what's the problem?

"Well, today I asked her if she'd given any thought to what I could do, and she turned real nasty and said, 'If you want to take over my job – if you think you can do it better – then you're welcome to it!' And she stomped away."

"Wow," John exclaimed.

"I was stunned," Pat said, sounding as if she were verging on tears.

Pat and John concluded that the best thing for Pat to do was simply nothing. If Georgia decided she wanted Pat's help, she could ask for it. Otherwise, Pat should just go on as if neither conversation had taken place.

John was surprised by Pat's account. He hadn't personally experienced any hostility from Georgia. One time she had told him he couldn't use the fellowship hall because it would somehow interfere with her opening exercises. John didn't think much of it, but Mike Wilkinson had come up to him at the time and said, "I can't believe she talked to you that way. I apologize for her behavior."

As time went on, John began to notice what he thought was a disturbing trait of Georgia's: She rarely attended the worship service. This bothered John in several ways. First, John was convinced that worship was a primary means of grace; for him, one could not be an effective leader in the church if he or she did not participate in community worship.

Second, Georgia's non-attendance in worship set a bad example for the children who were under her spiritual care. Often when Sunday School ended, Georgia would make a production of gathering up her materials and leaving the church building in full view of the kids getting their snacks and the parishioners coming in for worship.

Third, it was a snub of his efforts as a preacher and worship leader. To John, who worked hard to make worship a meaningful experience, it was a slap in the face.

Fourth, John saw Georgia's behavior as potentially detrimental to church growth. New attendees and new Christians might be discouraged by Georgia's example and question the authenticity of the church. John was concerned particularly about Jim and Lucy Erickson who had come to the church during the previous year and were becoming very involved and having a positive effect on the congregation. Their enthusiasm, devoutness, and generosity had noticeably raised the spirit of the church. John saw them as in tune with his vision for the church, but feared that if he didn't do something about Georgia, they would question his leadership.

John consulted with his mentor Gregg, an experienced clergy at a nearby church. "You've gotta wait a while," Gregg said. "You need to wait until you're confident the congregation is ready to move with you on the issue. Don't do anything without some good support."

While John personally would just as soon have ignored the whole thing, he didn't like waiting. As a pastor he felt he had to do something and waiting seemed cowardly. It wasn't long before a couple of incidents persuaded him it was time to take on Georgia.

It was early spring and the season to begin planning for Vacation Bible School. Several of the churches in town traditionally pooled their efforts and put together a community VBS which was held at John's church. The process had always been a relatively smooth one. However, this year John was surprised and embarrassed at a ministerial association meeting when one of the pastors said to him, "During our worship service last Sunday morning our office phone started ringing and it kept ringing from repeated callbacks until someone left the sanctuary and answered it. It was a woman from your church insisting that someone talk to her about Bible School. She was quite upset when we told her she was interrupting worship and that no one was available to talk to her."

The caller, of course, was Georgia. Skipping out on her own church's worship, she had rudely interrupted the service at another church. What in the world could she have been thinking of?

The final straw came for John when Lucy Erickson commented one evening, "I notice that Georgia doesn't come to church very often." Aha, thought John, here it comes. Actually Lucy didn't say much more in response to John's hesitant acknowledgement of Georgia's frequent absence from worship, but he was convinced she was concerned about the example Georgia was setting for the children. In reality, Lucy could've just as well been simply concerned about Georgia's health.

So John decided to call Georgia the next morning to confront her with her lack of attendance.

Morning came, and he did it – he picked up the phone and punched in Georgia's number.

"Hello."

"Hi, Georgia. This is Pastor John.

"Yes?"

"I'm calling because I've noticed you don't come to church very often."

"I come as often as I can. I don't really like that handholding thingee at the end."

"Well, I'm just concerned that it's not a very good example for the kids."

"You think I'm a bad example for the children?! Then I quit."

"No, no, I don't want you to quit. I just think the kids need to see you in church."

"I'll bring the Sunday School checkbook and other material over to the church this afternoon."

"Okay, if that's what you want to do."

It wasn't long before John heard about the phone calls. Georgia was calling every family in the congregation and telling them, "Pastor John says I'm a bad example for the children." When he was first informed he was worried – he hadn't anticipated this – so he asked his informant, "Did she say why I said that to her?" The answer was just what he wanted to hear: "Oh, yes – because she doesn't attend worship regularly."

"Bingo," said John. "No one can disagree with my assertion that it's a bad example for the Sunday School Superintendent to consistently skip church. Georgia is making my case for me." By this he was reassured that he had made the right decision. However, his confidence was short-lived.

During Wednesday night's youth gathering, Jim Erickson came up to him and said, "I've heard that someone telephoned Georgia and told her she needed to be in church more often."

"Yes."

"I hope no one from the church leadership made that call."

"I did."

"Really! We'll have to agree to disagree on this one."

John was stunned by Jim's reaction. He'd thought Jim would be one of his biggest supporters. He'd pegged Jim and Lucy as people who expected the pastor to insist on faithful practice of the spiritual disciplines by church leaders. What about Jim's favorite epistle, 1 Timothy, where the writer says, "If anyone wants to provide leadership in the church, good! But there are preconditions . . ."

Biblically, church leaders are held to a higher standard than the average Joe in the pew. John was befuddled and hurt that Jim wasn't giving his pastor greater support.

Sunday morning was a disaster. Attendance was way low and the mood was even lower. Pastor John had to do the Sunday School opening exercises because Doug, the Lay Leader and a teacher, declined to do so. It was clear Doug was letting John "stew in his own juices." Then Mike Williamson, the erstwhile Georgia critic, looked John in the eye and said, "It's terrible what's been done to Georgia." Nan, the organist, came up to him grumbling, "I knew it was too good to last, that you'd have to make a mistake sooner or later." Nan's husband Melvin echoed his wife's sentiments. The worship service itself was an hour of agony.

John couldn't understand what was happening. No one liked Georgia. How could they turn against him in defense of her? For the next several weeks – an eternity it seemed -- about all Jean and John talked about was the congregation's reaction to his Georgia initiative. They walked around and around the town most every night going over and over what had happened, trying to figure out what to do about it. The obsession didn't promote good family life. An additional stress point was the fact that Georgia's daughter was a best friend of their daughter Ann; fortunately both girls seemed to pretty much ignore the adult squabbling.

Thankfully there was a core of people supporting John. Primary among that group were Pat and Noll Richardson – Pat who'd had the Christmas program clash with Georgia and her husband who'd been Pastor-Parish Committee chairperson when John was appointed to the church. They and their family – Charlotte, Linda, Teddy, Liz – were Godsends. Other leaders in the church – a number of whom had met with John to tell him how wrong he was – continued to do their ministries well, so all was not lost. But most significantly, little growth, physical or spiritual, was going to occur with things as they were. As Pastor John put it, "The church is bleeding." Something needed to be done to staunch the flow.

* * * * *

Two events led to a cauterizing of the wound. First, Melvin, organist Nan's husband and Trustee chairperson, dropped into Pastor John's office one midweek afternoon.

"I don't know, John, if you are aware of Georgia's background."

"No, I don't guess I am."

"Well, I understand it was pretty rough. She came over here – when a child, I think – as a refugee from one of those Eastern European Communist countries. Don't know how much of her family made it out with her. Story is there was a lot of brutality. Given all she's been through, she's doing pretty darn good, it seems to me."

Blast it! thought John. Why do things have to get so complicated? What happened to black and white? Georgia obviously needed the ministry of the church as much or more than anyone else, but the church through Pastor John simply slaps her down. What a travesty! Yet, there are standards for being in leadership and one of the pastor's roles is to see that those standards are upheld. Isn't it? What was he to do?

The second and breakthrough event was brought about by the insightfulness of Lay Leader Doug Bauer.

Doug arranged to meet with Pastor John at the church office on a Saturday morning. "The time has come," he said, "to try to get this thing behind us."

"Any ideas how?" John asked.

"Yes. You have to take the initiative."

"And do what?"

"Apologize to Georgia. Now I don't mean you have to say you were wrong, at least not directly. I think, at this point, that it'd be enough for you to say you're sorry that it sounded like you thought she personally was a bad example when you didn't mean that at all. In fact, as you've thought and prayed over the past few weeks you've come to realize what a good example she's been to the kids through the years. You could then tell her how much the children miss her and something to the effect that the Sunday School is going down the tubes without her. Then ask her to please come back."

"I can do that," John replied without hesitation. "Do you think it'd be okay if I put it in a note to her? I think I could write it out more meaningfully than I could say it. Besides, the last telephone conversation Georgia and I had didn't go so well."

"Sure. Do it that way."

And that's what he did. He wrote the note and mailed it just before going to a denominational meeting for four days. On the third day, Doug called: "Georgia got your note and she's coming back! She'll be doing the opening exercises on Sunday."

"Hallelujah!" John exclaimed as he hung up the phone. "Thank you, God!" John knew, of course, that it hadn't been just his note. He was confident that Doug had gone to Georgia just as he had to John, and had paved the way for reconciliation. "Thank you also, God, for good lay leaders!"

* * * * *

The crisis had passed. The Sunday School was back on track. The joy returned to church. Yet John was still a little puzzled. Why had so many of the congregation deserted him on an issue where he was biblically correct? The answers came to John that summer in one of his seminary classes. It was right there on page ninety-eight of one of his texts, *Pastoral Stress* by Anthony G. Pappas: "When a pastor tries to fix something that isn't broken by the congregation's norm, he or she will not be applauded as a savior but derided as a meddler."

Why, thought John, couldn't I have read this before I made that fateful phone call to Georgia? Obviously, the great majority of the church thought the Sunday School was going splendidly, and when I criticized, I was meddling with what they saw as a good thing. (Of course, mentor Gregg had told him much the same thing and he hadn't listened.)

Insights offered in class by the professor shed further light: "You have to remember," the teacher said, "that you're just passing through while the church members are going to stay; it's their church, not yours. If you have trouble with a parishioner, keep in mind that she's one of them and you're not; they are going to be living with her after you're long gone."

John thought of Jesus' parable of the sower. A primary role of the pastor in a church is to sow good seed and help it grow as much as he or she can before he or she moves on. As with the farmer in another of Jesus' stories, some weeds are going to sprout also, but it's rarely the pastor's job to yank them out. Sometimes what looks like a weed is not.

Chapter 9

The Mission and the Table

October.

The golden fields of soybean and corn glistened with a light touch of frost. Jean and John were delighted with each rise to the top of a hill and with each plummet into the next valley as they sped along the country blacktop around sunrise. They were on their way to a local mission project. A group of approximately ten folks from the church were spending the Saturday doing repairs and improvements on the home of Eliza and her seven-year-old autistic grandson, Isaac. It was an old two-story farmhouse and church member Gary Ore had dedicated lots of hours to determining what needed to be done and then purchasing the supplies. They would be installing new rain gutters, fitting new ceiling fans and lights, hanging two new storm doors, building a deck railing, and painting an old detached garage. Material costs were borne by a local charitable organization with a focus on revitalizing existing housing.

Normally volunteers from other institutions such as banks and manufacturers would be participating, but given the location of the house, Pastor John's church group would be working solo. Lunch customarily would have been provided by the sponsoring agency but, again given the location, the work group would return to the church where congregational volunteers would serve them a hot meal. The situation, in John's eyes, couldn't have been better. Upon arrival at the house he had a very real sense of the presence of God.

John was determined to make this a better experience than his South Dakota trip of a number of years previous. So when everyone had arrived, the first thing he did was have them gather together, join hands, and pray. Reigning pooch Frodo joined in the prayer circle. Following prayer, they took a group picture and then turned to Gary for work assignments.

Gary offered John the task of building the railing, graciously showing him the lumber and other items associated with the project. John could discern no possible pattern or way that what he was shown could go together to form anything recognizable; he declined to undertake the enterprise. Gary suggested that John assist with the guttering, but John looked at the fascia two stories up, recalled his experience with ladders on the reservation, and again declined. Finally, Gary presented something John felt comfortable doing: Hanging the storm doors. At least there were instructions packed in with the door parts. John could usually follow a set of written instructions.

Two other persons were assigned to work with John on the storm doors. Taking off the old doors was very simple. When it came time to put up the new doors, the other two guys weren't interested in the instructions. They just plunged in and started mounting the frame. Predictably, after a few pieces had been installed, they ran into problems. Things just weren't fitting together as they should. While Dale and Roosevelt tried to figure out what to do, John seized the opportunity to read the instructions.

"Uh, Dale," John said a little hesitatingly, "according to the instructions the piece you're holding should have gone up first."

"No way!"

"Yes. And the pieces that are up there need to come down for now."

Dale and Roosevelt looked at the door, at each other, and then began to laugh. John was reminded of the time he and Jean had bought a four-strand retractable clothesline for their apartment. He'd opened the package, stretched the lines out, and, to his dismay, saw that most of the lines weren't taut but sagged terribly. He then opened the sheet of instructions which began with the following message in bold print: **"Now that you've totally screwed it up, this is what you need to do."** What a statement of the human condition! We're convinced we know what we're doing when often we don't have a clue.

Once the group commenced following the instructions, things went splendidly. By lunch time they had one door completely installed. Eliza was really excited about the new doors because so much cold air came in around the old ones that it had become increasingly difficult for her to heat the antique farmhouse.

Lunch was sacramental. There was bread. There was drink. There was hot soup. There was community. Christ was present. It seemed to John that their lunch was like he imagined the long ago feeding of the five thousand to be – people gathered together in the sacred presence of Jesus and one another enjoying the bounty of God's grace. He was so glad that they had been able to celebrate in this way. It highlighted their motivation for their day's deeds – love of God and love of neighbor.

The day finished up well. Everyone seemed to leave with a real sense of accomplishment. But there was more to come. A few days later they heard from the director of the sponsoring agency through Bonnie Johnson who had made the arrangements for the workday on behalf of the church. The director said, "From the very beginning this has been a unique project. When you called I had just hung up from a conversation with Eliza telling her that we didn't have any crews available to work in her area. After talking with you I was able to call Eliza back and say, 'It's a miracle!' even though I didn't believe in miracles. Then when I went out to the house on Saturday there was something different about the atmosphere – something more powerful than I had witnessed elsewhere. I can't put my finger on it, but it was almost magical."

About the same time as the call from the agency came to Bonnie, a thank-you note from Eliza arrived at the church. While she expressed much gratitude for the work done on her home, she gave her greatest thanks for the love that was shared with her, with Isaac, and with Frodo.

As Pastor John reflected on all that had happened, these words of Jesus came to him: "If anyone gives even a cup of cold water to one of these little ones because he is my disciple – I tell you the truth, he certainly will not lose his reward."

How true, John thought. How true.

Chapter 10

God's Not in Control

The sign again.

A controversial message – at least to some.

It read: "God is not always in control."

A Baptist pastor stopped by to quiz Pastor John about his theology and another clergy announced he was going to preach on the wrong-headedness of the message.

For John there was no controversy. Whenever he was tempted to subscribe to the God-is-in-control theory, he forced himself to think about Chelsea. It was always enough to disabuse himself of the notion.

Chelsea was seventeen.

She was by all accounts one of those people who brought joy to whomever she encountered. She was a senior yet related to freshmen as equal human beings, a real brave thing to do in a rigidly hierarchical American small town high school. There's at least one like her in most high school classes – the one who seems to be above the pettiness, who belongs to no clique but is tacitly accepted by all the groups, who is quite simply respected – the one who seems to embody the spirit of the school and is somehow assumed by all to be destined for success and to live life well.

On that Tuesday night before Thanksgiving Chelsea had been at the basketball game. Following the game a gathering was happening at the local bowling alley. Chelsea bid her friends farewell, promising to meet them at the lanes.

Why she did what she did no one can know for sure. Was she in a hurry because she just didn't want to miss any of the fun? Was she distracted by something and simply not paying close enough attention? Did she misjudge the circumstances?

In any event, she pulled out from the stop sign into the path of a semi tractor-trailer rig which was traveling at fifty-five miles per hour. Try as he did, there was no way the driver could get the rig halted. It literally ran over Chelsea's little car smashing metal, bone, and flesh. What pain she must have experienced! What agony for the trucker! To John it was clear: The God revealed in Jesus was not in control of what happened that night at that intersection. Such a God would never will such a horrific thing.

* * * * *

"But doesn't the Bible teach us that God is sovereign and that all things – good and evil -- happen through his providential activity?" one pastor challenged.

"Not at all," John responded. "As early in the biblical text as Genesis 1: 28, God -- out of divine love -- surrendered control and gave human beings responsibility for the welfare of the planet and the creatures on it. Included in that freedom is the possibility of error such as miscalculating the speed and distance of an approaching semi."

"Okay, assuming that you are correct in that assertion, how do you account for natural disasters? Humans can't control those."

"Well," John continued, "perhaps more of those so-called natural disasters are the result of human activity than we care to admit. And people have done much to control the impact of natural forces through dams, levees, building codes, and such. More to the point is the fact that Creation is ongoing. God set in motion a process that is not yet completed – a process which involves earthquakes and floods, tornadoes and hurricanes, volcanoes and fire. But

I'm confident God is not sending hurricanes to places like New Orleans to punish people."

* * * * *

John's parsonage was only a short distance from the intersection where Chelsea's accident occurred. Normally he would have heard the sirens, but that Tuesday night was different. He had decided not to work but to spend time with his daughter Ann watching a movie; therefore, at the time of the event they were ensconced in the TV room with the sound of the video drowning out all external noise. It wasn't until he received a telephone call from a parishioner the next morning that John knew what had happened. He promptly called the high school to see what he could do to help. The principal asked him to come to the school to be available to the students.

It was a terrible day. And most terrible was when a young couple brought Chelsea's eight-year-old cousin to him. She had a question – a question that John found unanswerable: "I prayed all the way to the hospital for Chelsea to not die. But when we got there, she was dead. Why didn't God answer my prayer?"

"Well, sometimes God has other purposes that we can't see," John said, stumbling over his words. "It's a mystery to us. Sometimes it's just time for a life to end for reasons we don't know or understand. The Bible tells us that there is a time for everything – a time to live and a time to die -- and that only God knows the schedule. But God promises to bring good out of all things for us who love God." John knew his answer was inadequate. He knew that he only half-believed some of it. But it was all he had and that fact made him feel totally inadequate as a pastor. He grieved that he was not capable of bringing some comfort to that little girl.

Chelsea's funeral was a Catholic one, but it was held at Pastor John's United Methodist church because it had the greatest seating capacity of the local churches. John's congregation really stepped up as the body of Christ and did all they could for Chelsea's family. Not only did they offer the use of the building with no demand that their pastor have a part in the service, but they prepared and served the funeral luncheon. John was really proud of them.

Following the service and while the family and others were at the cemetery for Chelsea's interment, John and others set up the tables and chairs for the luncheon. They finished before people got back and some of them were sitting in the fellowship hall having coffee, noting that it was lightly raining. They hadn't been sitting there long when one of the children, little Jeanie, came running in saying, "There's a big rainbow in the sky." Everyone got up and went to the windows, and sure enough there was a beautiful rainbow arcing across the sky. The folks at the cemetery saw it too.

The rainbow announced by Jeanie said it all, John often thought. God doesn't necessarily will things to happen, but God is present and promises to empower us to establish justice, to grant mercy, to provide for the needy, to care for and heal the sick, to be peacemakers, to advance God's kingdom on earth. God will always be a present help, but we are the first responders in our world. John just hoped that someday Chelsea's little cousin would come to understand this and to take comfort in it.

* * * * *

The sign was not changed.

Chapter 11

Children's Time

Children's Time is, for many pastors, one of the most loved and most feared exercises of Sunday morning. It can be the highlight of the service or it can crash and burn. Who can predict what those tykes are going to do or how they're going to respond? Who knows for sure how the pastor's carefully planned demonstration will come together?

Pastor John shared the ambivalence. For him, Children's Time was like a high wire act without a net. And he'd had his share of slipping off the wire. For example, there was the apple debacle.

The message was the importance of seeds – literal and metaphorical. The approach was to hold up an apple and ask the children from whence it came. After getting past "grocery store" to "tree" the next question was, "Where does the tree come from?" Once the answer "seeds" was proposed, then the inquiry was, "Where do the seeds come from?" Ideally, someone would come up with, "Inside the apple." Then the apple would be cut and the seeds shown, at which point John would say something like, "Just as this apple has seeds inside to spread more trees across the land, we have the seeds of love within us and God wants us to scatter them through our kindnesses toward others."

Everything went fine until he cut the apple. There were no seeds. He had cut it the wrong way, something he didn't realize until much later. Blessedly, several of the school teachers in the congregation expressed their sympathy at the end of the service. They too had experienced such failures in the classroom.

* * * * *

Then there was the story of Jonah – a lesson on obedience to God's will. When God tells you to go someplace and do something, you'd better do it or you might end up in some much worse place, like the belly of a whale. Things went splendidly until little Paris announced, "And the whale was purple!" Pastor John, in a silly effort to maintain biblical accuracy, responded to Paris: "Well, actually we don't know what color the whale was; the Bible doesn't tell us that."

Paris was quite taken aback by John's temerity. "It was purple – a purple whale," Paris insisted. "I can show you. I'll bring my book next Sunday."

"That'd be great," John conceded. "Let's pray."

The following Sunday Paris was ready. When Pastor John called for the children to come forward, Paris marched up proudly, holding her book. It was a children's edition of the story of Jonah. And right on the cover was a picture of the whale – a big, purple whale!

"See," Paris said. "Jonah's whale was purple!"

Having been confronted with unassailable documentary proof, the fruit of a child's diligent research, John had no choice but to again concede the point. "So it appears," John replied. "I never knew.

"Well," Paris continued, "so you don't ever forget, you can keep the book."

For the remainder of John's time at that church, the book of Jonah's purple whale sat conspicuously on a shelf of his office bookcase so all could know the truth.

* * * * *

There were always some parents who questioned the church's practice of serving communion to the children.

The dialogue he usually had with them went something like this:

Parent: "The children just don't understand it."

John: "Neither do the adults. Neither do any of us. It's supposed to be a mystery."

Parent: "Well, the kids just don't know at all what it's about and how to behave."

John: "I have to differ. I think the children very much sense that something truly sacred is going on. I think they experience the presence of God even though they, like us, can't really articulate it. By observing how the adults behave, they know communion is special. They get a sense of the holy."

Parent: "Maybe so. But I still think there ought to at least be a class or something for them to learn about communion."

John thought about holding a class, but he was skeptical about the potential attendance. He foresaw scheduling a time and only a couple of children being brought. Then he had a stroke of genius! He would offer instruction during Sunday worship. In fact, the service would be centered upon the Children's Time where the topic would be Holy Communion. That time would pre-empt the sermon and become the message for everyone that morning.

When the appointed Sunday came, the chancel was occupied by a long table designed to evoke an image of the Last Supper. The children gathered on the chancel steps as usual, and John talked to them about the Passover.

"A very long time ago, many years before the time of Jesus, the Hebrew people were slaves in the country of Egypt. They called out to God to be set free, God heard them, and God sent the man Moses to go tell the Egyptian king to let God's people go. Remember this story?"

"Yes," one of the children quickly responded, and with an abundance of hand motions continued: "Pharaoh said, 'No! Absolutely not!' and so God got mad and turned the river to blood and sent a bunch of plagues – jumping frogs, biting gnats, buzzing flies, boils on the skin, big hailstones, grasshoppers that ate up all the crops – and he made the farm animals die and then lots of the Egyptian children died. After the children died, Pharaoh said the Hebrews could go away."

"Exactly. Very good!" Pastor John commended. "And before the final plague, Moses told the Hebrew people to get ready to flee Egypt by making bread to take with them. Since they were in a big hurry, the bread had to be unleavened – flat like a cracker – because there wasn't enough time to let it rise. That night before leaving Egypt, Hebrew families gathered in their houses and ate a supper of roasted lamb and unleavened bread. That supper came to be called the Passover meal because God passed over the houses of the Hebrews and the children in those houses didn't die. From then until now, at the same time every year, Jewish people all over the world have a Passover meal to remember the night the Hebrew children were spared and the Hebrew people were freed from slavery in Egypt. Now let us go gather around the table up here."

Once everyone was seated around the table, John said: "On the night before he died on the cross, Jesus and his disciples got together in an upstairs room in a rich man's house to have their Passover meal, for it was that time of year. But Jesus changed some things. When they ate the unleavened bread, he said, 'This is my body given for you; eat it to remember me.' And then when they drank the wine, he said, 'This is my blood shed for you; drink it in remembrance of me.' And this is what we do when we have Holy Communion every month. We remember Jesus and what he taught, and how he lived, and how he died for us. When we do this, Jesus draws especially close to us."

"Pastor!" Johnny shouted as his hand shot up. "Did Jesus want to die?"

Wow, thought John, they're actually listening and taking all this in.

"No, Johnny, I don't think Jesus wanted to die at all. I think Jesus loved life and would've wanted very much to go on living. He knew that God had told the Hebrew people to 'choose life'.

"But Jesus also knew that the people who opposed him – very powerful people – were going to try to kill him. And he knew he had to love them, not strike back, because God is Love. That's what he had come to show everyone, that God is Love. That's what he had spent all that time teaching his disciples – to meet violence with love. To be true to his message of love, he had to let them hang him on the cross if that's what they were determined to do.

"But he also knew that God would not desert him, and would bring him back from the dead, as God would do for all people who love. So, even though he didn't want to die, he willingly died to show us that Love always wins.

"So let us each take a piece of the unleavened bread, which is also called matzo, and eat."

Unfortunately, John had not tasted it beforehand. It was like eating cardboard or wood chips. It was awful! The kids would certainly remember this, he thought. So would the entire congregation since they were served the same.

As quickly as possible, John poured the glasses of grape juice and said, "As Jesus commanded, let us drink of the juice that represents the blood he shed for us. Amen."

For as long as John served that church, the people spoke of the awful unleavened bread and the very special communion with the children.

* * * * *

Randy and his family began attending the church upon their move to the community. At the time, Randy was probably somewhere around four or five years of age. During Children's Time, Randy was always intensely attentive, seemingly hanging onto every word Pastor John said. John, of course, was flattered that he so skillfully attracted Randy's interest with his finely-crafted messages. However, as he would soon learn, the interest was prompted, at least in part, by a misunderstanding.

The revelation came on a Sunday morning as folks were coming into the church. John was in the narthex greeting people upon their arrival. When Randy and his family came in the door, Randy spotted John right off, and enthusiastically shouted, "Hi, God!"

Ahh. It became clear. Randy was in awe of John because he was laboring under the misconception that John was God. "No, no," Randy's mother said. "Pastor John tells us about God, but he's not God." John kinda hated to give up the position, but he affirmed what Randy's mom had said. Randy continued to participate in Children's Time, even becoming a little more vocal. (It's a little more comfortable to speak when you're just talking to a pastor and not God face-to-face.)

Pastor John, on the other hand, endured no end of razzing from Judy, the finance committee chair and office assistant, who witnessed John's whole encounter with Randy and his family. She quickly began holding him to a much higher standard. As she put it, "If you're going to go around making the kids think you are God, then you're going to have to measure up!"

* * * * *

Children's Time: A little bit of stress, a fair amount of embarrassment, a lot of fumbling, and often the best part of the service.

Chapter 12

David

He called during lunch on Saturday. The question was: "Do you have any extra garbage bags I could use?"

Pastor John wasn't particularly surprised by the question. When Jean and he had visited David and his boy Brent, David had spoken of his need to clear all the accumulated trash out of his apartment. Apparently, he was undertaking the project that day.

"What size?"

"Large, I guess."

John took a moment to look under the kitchen sink. "Got 'em. We'll drop the box off after lunch."

John had first encountered David when David dropped into the fellowship hall one Sunday while the early-morning arrivers were gathered for their coffee and conversation. For John it was always an easing-into-the-day time. He enjoyed the comfort of it. David was warmly welcomed, offered coffee and donut, hugged by the choir director, and given medical advice by the attending physician.

"You live here in town, David?"

"Yeah. Down on Main Street. Got an apartment in the back of the house next to that church."

"Grow up around here?"

"No. Down south. Got married to a girl from up around here. Moved to her town a few years ago. Was great for a while, but ended up divorced."

"Got any children?"

"Yeah, Brent. He's five. His mother has him right now, but he lives with me. She doesn't really want him much. Interferes with her new family, I guess."

"You working?"

"Uh-huh. Got a job welding in a little shop up river. Doesn't pay much, but it's better 'n nothing."

"Well, welcome to the church. Let me know if there's anything we can do for you."

"I'd like to talk with you about some stuff sometime."

"That'd be fine. Just drop by during the week. Best if you call first to make sure I'm here or to find out when I will be."

A week or two later, David and Brent stopped by the parsonage around supper time. John had just gotten home. The purpose of the visit was financial.

"Pastor John, I need a little gas money. I don't have enough gas to get to work tomorrow. It's payday, so I can give it back to you tomorrow night."

"How much do you need?"

"Ten or so ought to do it."

"Here's twenty."

"Thanks. Get it back to you tomorrow."

"Don't worry about it. Keep the money so you'll have gas next week."

"Well, thanks again. I'd still like to sit down and talk with you sometime when you got a chance."

At that point Brent burst back into the room, having just come up from the basement where Jean had taken him to entertain him so David and John could talk.

"Hey, Dad, they've got lots of cool stuff down there! All kinds of board games and other stuff. Can I come back and play sometime?"

"That's a great idea, Brent," John said. "You could come and stay with Jean for a time while your dad and I do some other things." He glanced over at David who appeared to think the suggestion was okay. "How about Tuesday around six, after you're off work, David?"

"I guess so," David replied.

"Okay, it's set."

"Why don't you two stay for supper tonight?" Jean asked. "We've got plenty and it's almost ready."

"Sure," John affirmed.

"We better not," David said. "I've got stuff we need to use at home."

"Well, suit yourself," Jean said. "We'd love to have you stay."

"We should go."

And they left.

* * * * *

David and Brent didn't show up on Tuesday. A week or so later both of them came to John's office door and David again asked for some gas money. He had a paycheck with him, but said there was no place open where he could cash it. Given the presence of Brent, it was impossible for John and David to have any sort of meaningful discussion about David's situation. Brent was particularly keyed-up, pulling things off the bookshelves and constantly interrupting and making demands on David. So Pastor John handed over some dollars out of a petty cash fund and wished them well. He again encouraged David to make arrangements to come in by himself.

David then pretty much dropped out of sight for a month or two. John suspected, however, that David had come to the house one snowy Friday morning. It was John's day off and he and Jean were sleeping-in – until Jean awakened him with: "There's somebody knocking on the patio door." John listened for a few moments then got up, put on his robe, and trekked to the door.

"No one there," he reported upon his return to the bedroom. "But there were some footprints in the snow leading up to the door. Whoever it was obviously gave up."

When John went outside later that morning, he saw a single set of tire tracks in the driveway and boot-sized footsteps in the snow. His first thought was that the visitor was David seeking money; he expressed his second to Jean like this: "You would think if he wanted money he would have at least shoveled the sidewalk. The shovel is right there by the door. He couldn't have missed it. I fear our friend David is somewhat lazy."

* * * * *

Following the snowy Friday episode, John didn't give much thought to David. Over the years he had become accustomed to people drifting in and out of the church. His philosophy was that as pastor he had the primary responsibility of making the church as welcoming, inviting, and meaningful as possible, and that he couldn't personally devote a lot of time to pursuing folks. Ultimately, however, he was prompted by a parishioner to make an effort to check up on David and Brent; she had concerns about their well-being. She had heard that David had severe, life-threatening, medical problems, that he had lost his job because of absenteeism, that his truck had been repossessed, and that Brent was not attending his kindergarten class.

So one Sunday evening, John and Jean went down to David's place.

"Hi, David," John said as David admitted them into the kitchen. "We hadn't seen you for a while so we thought we'd come down and see how you're doing."

"Oh, okay, I guess."

"Well, we heard that you were seriously ill."

"No, not really. I do get migraines and I've had quite a few lately."

"How about your job? Are you still able to work?"

"I got laid off. They didn't have any more work for me to do. It always gets slow for them in the winter."

"Can you get unemployment comp?"

"I don't know."

"You probably should check it out."

"Yeah, but I don't have a way to get there. I had to give the truck back."

"Jean and I would be happy to give you a lift to the unemployment office and wherever you have to go to get the help you need."

Thus Jean and John began spending a fair amount of time shuttling David around, mostly to clinics, emergency rooms, and pharmacies. On occasion, when they didn't need it for other purposes, they loaned him their car. Other folks in the church also pitched in to provide transportation for David, and there was the occasional box of food delivered to his apartment.

* * * * *

After lunch on the aforementioned Saturday, John and Jean headed down to David's place with a box of garbage bags. When they got there they discovered that David didn't want the bags for garbage, but for moving out.

"I'm going to have to go to a shelter," David announced as they stood in the kitchen.

"Oh," John replied. "Why's that?" he asked, confident that he knew the answer.

"The landlord told me to be out by Monday. I owe a couple of months' rent."

"What about Brent?"

"I guess I'll call his mom and tell her she's going to have to come and get him."

"What shelter are you going to?"

"I don't know. I thought I'd call and see where there's space. I still have a little time on my phone."

"How're you going to get there?"

"Walk and hitch a ride if I can."

"Well, let us know when you're ready and we'll give you a lift. Tell you what, we'll just drop back by this evening and see what you've worked out.

"Okay."

"See you then. See you later, Brent," John called into the living room where Brent had been glued to the television screen the entire time John and Jean had been there.

"Bye."

Pastor John and Jean drove on into the city to complete some errands. They stopped for coffee at their favorite bookstore, and as they were sitting there reading, Jean looked up at John and said, "I've been thinking that maybe we should invite David to stay with us. We have plenty of room since Ann moved out on her own. David could have her old room and Brent could have the guest room."

"I've been contemplating that too," John answered. "It seems to be something Jesus would have us do. It could certainly be good for Brent. Hopefully we could help him get back to regular attendance at school. And he'd have a nice yard to play in, not to mention some better meals, I'm sure."

"Yes. It'd be good for Brent, particularly if what David says about his mother not wanting him is true."

"We'd have to insist that David seek the public assistance he's entitled to. He needs to get enrolled for food stamps so he can help get nutritious food for Brent, and he's probably eligible for medical assistance if he'd just apply. I have a feeling that he's just running up all sorts of bills for these ER visits and that's going to really bog him down later if he gets work."

"That's another thing," Jean interposed. "Work. If he's got a secure place for Brent and him to live and eat, he should be able to focus on looking for work so he can begin saving some money to get his own place again."

"That's right. I've been thinking about that. How is he going to be able to get around to look for work and to get to and from a job if he actually acquires one? The church is planning to get rid of the church van. It's just not reliable enough to haul kids and youth around in, and we're tired of the constant repair bills. Maybe I could get the trustees to just give it to David. With some tender, loving care, it could probably serve him well for a decent period of time. We could have it serviced and take care of any safety issues before we give it to him, and I think the Missions Team might be able to front a few months of insurance for him."

"Okay, let's do it. But let's wait until Monday to move him in. I'd like a day to adjust to the idea."

"Makes sense. Shall we go see if he wants to do it?"

When they got back to David's place, they found he hadn't made any progress locating a shelter, hadn't called Brent's mother about taking him, and hadn't filled any bags. While this struck John as irresponsible, he decided it was at least partially good given what he and Jean were going to propose.

"David," John began, "we'd like for you and Brent to come live with us for a time while you try to get back on your feet. We have plenty of room and you might as well use it. What do you think."

"Brent," David shouted into the living room, "would you like to go live with Pastor John and Jean?"

Brent came into the kitchen. "Can we really? That'd be cool."

"It sounds like he wants to," Jean said.

"There are two primary conditions," John continued. First, Brent has to go to school every day unless he's sick. Second, both of you have to attend church on Sunday. Not only do I think it'd be good for you, I couldn't justify to the people of the church your living in their parsonage and not coming to worship."

"No problems there," David assured them. "We really appreciate what you're doing."

"Okay, then it's set," John said. "We'll come down Monday and pick you and your stuff up."

The church was very supportive of the efforts John and Jean were making in regard to David and Brent. The trustees pitched in and had the old van serviced and then signed the title over to David. People donated to a special fund set up to pay for title transfer and registration and to cover three months of liability insurance. David was welcomed into the church and the children's ministry people embraced Brent as if he'd been with them always. Brent attended school every day and his teacher commented what a difference it made in his performance. Through a referral by a church member, David got a decent welding and general maintenance job with a local farmers' co-op. And for a long-lasting contribution, David dug up a sizable area of sod to make a place for a parsonage vegetable garden. All-in-all, John and Jean were feeling pretty good about what the church and they had accomplished, and how David and Brent seemed to be flourishing.

But it wasn't very long before the arrangement began to crumble.

David demonstrated a total irresponsibility in regard to the van. One morning John noticed and pointed out to David that there was something hanging down under the van and recommended that he check it out. David ignored John's suggestion. He ignored it until one morning the van wouldn't start and John had to take him to work. It turned out that the thing hanging down was the belt that was designed to keep the alternator running and the battery charged, among other things. Fortunately, no great damage was done. The mechanic who repaired the vehicle did report, however, that the oil level was apparently not being checked and that it was dangerously low.

When John and Jean indicated that Brent should not be up running around the house until midnight when he had school in the mornings, David took to holing up in his room with Brent from right after supper until they fell asleep. Mostly, it seemed, they lay in the bed and watched movies on TV. Brent never used the room Jean had specially fixed-up for him; he slept with David, which John did not think was good for either one of them.

Then David began claiming that he was experiencing the migraines again. He started missing work and staying in bed most of the day. Jean would have to go into the room and wake Brent for school.

The breaking point came with Easter. David and Brent skipped the Easter services – both the sunrise and late morning services – and the breakfast in-between the two where John and Jean had hoped David would help out. Then – the clincher for John – David was rude toward Jean and John's daughter Ann during Easter dinner. This is where John lost his composure and verbally attacked David, using language he thought he had put away years ago.

As soon as Ann went out the door to return to her apartment, and Jean went out to the car ahead of him to leave on their Easter week vacation, John turned to David and shouted, "How dare you treat my daughter in such a way! She tried to be kind and gracious toward you and you did everything but spit in her face!"

"I was trying not to interfere with family."

"The hell you were! You were just being obnoxious and mean-spirited. I can't believe anyone would behave in such a manner as a guest in someone's home."

"I didn't want to get in the way."

"And why weren't you in church this morning? You know that's a condition of your staying here."

"I just didn't think I'd fit in."

"Bullshit!" You were just too damned lazy to get your ass out of bed and get it over there."

With that, John exited, slamming the door behind him, and got into the car.

Simply put, David did not conform to many of Pastor John's culturally-influenced expectations and that infuriated John. John realized that he was probably trying too hard to impose his social values on David, but he also thought: How in the world is David going to create a better life for himself and Brent if he doesn't do a better job of relating to people?

At the beginning of the arrangement, Jean and John told David that he and Brent would have to leave for a couple of weeks in July when their daughter and granddaughter from California came to visit. They would probably have relented and not required David and Brent to vacate if the Easter incidents hadn't happened. But John wasn't about to expose his other daughter to the same treatment as David had given to daughter Ann.

Several church families offered to take David and Brent in for the couple of weeks, but David didn't follow up on any of the invitations. Instead, he hooked up with a woman from church and Pastor John never saw David, Brent, or the woman again. Except for one brief moment several weeks later when David caught him in the fellowship hall of the church and asked for some gas money. John quickly and coldly rejected the request.

* * * * *

The poor. Pastor John firmly believed that Jesus expressed a special love for the poor. But was David one of those? John struggled with the question. He thought of his erstwhile conviction that given a decent opportunity, everyone would be willing to work. Experience had taught him: Not so much. But does it matter? There is often a level of choice in poverty, but also much if not all of the time the poor are the discards of social, cultural, economic machines much older and larger than they. When Jesus said, "You will always have the poor with you," did he mean because we will always be creating them until we make the fundamental systemic changes we need to make?

In retrospect, Pastor John was confident of one thing: David would've had more of a chance if he had gone to one of the decent shelters in the area. John and Jean would have done him more of a service if they had taken him to one of those shelters. And Brent? His dad was not really good for him. The values he was teaching him were not positive and would not help him find a productive place in the world. Brent would be better off somewhere else.

Jesus invites the children of the world to come to him. Pastor John prayed that Brent could be in a place to hear and accept the invitation.

Chapter 13

Lunch to Go

Pastor John was preparing to enter his car when the man's silhouette suddenly appeared in the frame of the open overhead door. The brightness of the outside light prevented John from seeing the man's features, but he could make out that he was quite large, and that was a little frightening to John.

"Are you the pastor here?" the man asked as he stepped through the door and into the garage.

"Yes, I am."

"I rang the bell at the house but no one answered."

"Can't hear it out here. What can I do for you?"

"Could you spare a few bucks so I could get some lunch?"

John looked at the man's dirty clothes and figured he was riding the rails – a transient. The tracks cut right through town about three blocks west of the parsonage. Occasionally a freight would stop to drop off some cars and a rider would come looking for something to eat.

* * * * *

A childhood memory suddenly popped into John's head. He was playing on the kitchen floor when a knock rattled the back door. He looked up at his mother who was standing at the sink. "Wonder who that could be," she said as she dried her hands on the dish towel. She walked over to the door and opened it. A skinny bearded man stood there. He said, "Howdy, ma'am. Best of the day to you. Wonder if you might have a sandwich or something to spare."

"Let me check," she replied as she closed the door.

"Who was it, Mother?"

"Oh, just an old hobo from the railroad. I'm going to make him a bologna sandwich."

John remembered standing up and watching his mother make the sandwich. It was a larger sandwich than she usually made – two slices of bologna rather than one, a whole slice of cheese rather than half. She wrapped it in waxed paper and on her way to the door stopped to pour the man a cup of coffee from the pot she always had on the stove. "Give him one of your cookies," he recalled saying.

"That's a good idea, Johnny."

The man sat on the back step and ate the lunch John's mother had provided. He ate slowly, completely chewing each bite before swallowing and taking another. The same with the coffee – no gulping, but a slow sipping between the bites of sandwich. He stood up to leave, stuffed the waxed paper into one of his pants pockets, took the final swig of coffee, bent to set the empty cup on the step, and walked away.

"Why didn't he sit at our table?" Johnny asked his mother.

"Oh, he would have been too uncomfortable doing that."

* * * * *

John shook his head to clear his thoughts and focused on the man before him. "Sure," he said, "let's walk down to the diner and you can order what you want."

The diner was only a couple of blocks away. John walked around the man and through the door, indicating that his guest should follow. As they walked along, John said, "My name is John," and the man replied, "I'm Matthew and I'm much obliged for your kindness."

John and Matthew arrived at the diner and took seats on the stools at the short counter that ran straight ahead from the entry door. Most of the tables were occupied by chatting townsfolks.

"Hi, Jeanie," John said to the waitress behind the counter.

"Hello, Pastor. What can I do for you?"

"We'll have a couple of coffees and Matthew here needs to order lunch."

"Okay, what would you like?" Jeanie asked, looking at Matthew.

"A cheeseburger."

"Fries with that?"

"Uhh –"

"Sure," John interjected. "And what kind of pie do you have today?"

"Apple, peach, and coconut cream."

"Which do you prefer, Matthew?"

"Apple, I guess."

"Is this for here or to go?"

John fully intended to say "here" but Matthew was quicker with a "to go."

"I'll get this right up for you," Jeanie said as she turned toward the kitchen.

John recalled the words of his mother when he asked why the man didn't eat at their table: "He would've been too uncomfortable." He understood now. His mom's hobo and his transient came from worlds different than theirs. Their guests were not interested in hearing about the wonders of a settled life and even less desirous of answering probing questions about their own peripatetic ways.

He also thought of some scripture. First: "Do not neglect to show hospitality to strangers for some have entertained angels unaware." Then Jesus' conversation with the blessed:

"When I was hungry, you gave me something to eat."

"When did we give you something to eat?"

"When you gave it to one of the least of these."

So, Matthew sitting silently next to him awaiting his to-go sack could be an angel or even Jesus himself. Well, if that's the case, it's certainly a good thing I'm getting him some lunch, John concluded.

"Where you headed?" John asked, unable to bear the silence any longer and thinking it's better to ask a man where he's going than where he's been.

"To the melon fields – Decker, Indiana, Muscatine, Iowa. It's good work."

"Here's your coffee," Jeanie said, setting the Styrofoam cups in front of them.

"I like picking fruit," Matthew continued. "They usually make me a cutter in the watermelon fields – a little easier. It's good eating when a melon gets busted open, you know."

The burger, fries, and pie arrived neatly placed in a brown paper sack. Matthew rose, took hold of the sack in one hand and the coffee cup in the other, said "Thank you, Pastor," and left.

As John was paying, Gary, the restaurant owner, commented, "Those damn hobos are sure a problem coming around here expecting a handout."

Hobo. John hadn't heard that word used like that since he was a boy and his mother said it. "Oh, I don't know, Gary," he said, "I think he might've been an angel – or maybe Jesus."

"Whatever," Gary said as he closed the register drawer.

As he left the restaurant, John could see Matthew walking along toward the railroad tracks. Well, he thought, that certainly depleted my funds for this week, but it was worth it, I think. I feel pretty good.

* * * * *

That night, as he was getting ready for bed, John reached into his pants pockets to empty them. "What's this?" he mumbled as he felt a piece of paper stuffed into the left-side pocket. He pulled it out. It was a twenty-dollar bill. "Now how did that get there?"

Chapter 14

Hot August Night

It had been a scorcher of a day and the evening was bringing little remission. The tiny office was filled way beyond its capacity by the six people sitting in the folding chairs. The one window faced west where the sun remained powerful in the August sky. The air conditioner rattled in its window mounting; already defeated by the humidity, it continued to bravely struggle against the temperature. The people in the room were sweating, fanning themselves with the papers that had been circulated among them, wiping their faces with handkerchiefs and tissues. The occasion was the examination of Pastor John and wife Jean.

The denominational authorities had appointed John pastor of the church. This session was designed to give the Pastor-Parish Relations Committee members an opportunity to meet John and his family and for them to in turn learn more about the church and its people. However, oftentimes the gathering was viewed by a committee as a job interview; such was the case here. So, before it was over, John's sweating was symptomatic of more than the heat.

The questions weren't unfair, just penetrating: Why do you want to be a pastor? Why did you leave your previous profession? Do you think you can live in a small town after so many years of city life? Can you live on what we can pay you? How can you help us grow? Will you stay?

The interrogation didn't take place in just one sitting; there were several. A few questions would be asked, John and Jean would answer and then be excused while the committee members and the district superintendent conferred. The times of exclusion gave John and Jean an opportunity to check up on the kids, eighteen-year-old Laura and twelve-year-old Ann. The children had already served their function of being introduced and were no longer a recognized part of the proceedings. Having spent their time thoroughly exploring the 1960's church building, they gave John and Jean several guided tours into its recesses.

Noll, the chair of the committee, was an engineer by profession. The day before the meeting had been the day of his elder daughter's wedding, so he brought a spirit of joy to the room as well as his engineer's sense of orderliness and reason.

Ed was a farm co-op manager and an inventor. He had recently invented a dust control device for his co-op's elevators. One of his daughters was facing brain surgery at the end of the month. He brought the excitement of success tempered by the agony of his child's uncertain future.

Lynne was a bubbly mother of two who worked as a florist at a local shop. She taught one of the Sunday School classes and brought a youthful exuberance to the gathering.

It became clear to John and Jean that the committee did not wish for them to become the church's pastoral family. Not that the members personally disliked them, but for some reason they didn't find them satisfactory. When they were called back into the room for the last time, the emphasis was on healing. How was John going to heal the hurt the people of the church had experienced as a result of the prior pastor's sudden departure?

What could one say in answer to such a question? By listening? By preaching? Pastoral care can be delivered in so many ways, thought John. In his answer, he focused upon the healing power of worship – of the community of faith gathering together week after week to be in the presence of one another and God. It was, he knew, a response drawn from the mystical side of Christianity, but one to which he hoped they could relate.

Lynne was the first to speak. "Is this not," she said, "a matter of our trust in God? I feel that John and Jean have been brought to us by God and that we should trust that God knows what is good for our church."

"Amen!" Ed exclaimed."

They were in.

In the parking lot, after the committee members had driven away, the district superintendent told John and Jean: "They wanted someone with more experience, and I said to them, 'For what you're paying, you're not going to get it.'" True as the DS's statement might have been, John was confident he now understood what Noll, Ed, and Lynne wished to know, what their real question was: "Will you love us?"

As they traveled through Galesburg on the way home, Jean and John decided it was time to show some love to their children. They stopped at one of those gas station / convenience stores and turned Ann and Laura loose to get whatever snacks they wanted. They came back with Three Musketeers bars and Jolly Ranchers, Squirts and Mountain Dews, Doritos and Pringles. Blessedly, the district superintendent also pulled in and insisted on paying for all the treats.

* * * * *

Over the next few weeks, as he prepared to assume the pastorate, John struggled with the question of love. How does a pastor go about loving a congregation? he asked himself. The answer that came to him was quite simple: Do your job. So that became his approach – doing those things a pastor is supposed to do:

Show up for worship on Sunday mornings. On time. Preferably early.

Prepare a message. Work on it. Make it the very best you can.

Shake hands with people after the service. Hug the huggers.

Visit people in the hospital. Pray.

Sit with families whose loved ones are undergoing surgery. Pray.

Visit those stuck at home or in a care facility. Pray.

Make Children's Time important.

Be around.

Admit what you're not good at doing.

Invest yourself in the weddings and funerals.

A couple of months later, at coffee time, Noll came up to John and said to him, "I'm glad you're here. I had my doubts, but they're gone now. We couldn't ask for a better pastor. Welcome."

* * * * *

A Banner Day

Jean found her own ways to demonstrate love. Interestingly, it was in connection with the annual financial campaign that she perhaps made her earliest and most visible statement of love.

Many pastors don't like to talk about money. Most congregations don't like to hear the pastor talking about money. Pastor John was well-aware of all this, so he was approaching his first campaign with a certain measure of trepidation. How can I do this? he prayed.

The primary scripture John chose for the drive was Malachi 3: 8-10. One weekday morning he was sitting in a pew doing his prayers. He looked around the sanctuary – at the large black iron cross mounted above the altar, at the colorful cloth banners hanging on either side of the cross, at the altar itself with the large Bible open to one of the psalms, at the pulpit, and at the lectern. What captured his attention, however, was the indirect lighting that ran around the sanctuary. The light fixtures themselves were concealed by wood panels approximately twelve inches in width that ran underneath them and alongside them, forming a trough that directed the rays of light upward onto the cathedral ceiling of the nave. John's inspiration: Continuous feed computer paper with the scripture written on it could be attached to that wood screening. John's second inspiration: Jean would be very good at doing that.

So, Jean did a paper banner that stretched around three sides of the sanctuary. The letters were large red ones outlined in black. They read:

> **Will anyone rob God? Yet you are robbing me! How? In your tithes and offerings. Bring the full tithe in and put me to the test. See if I will not open the windows of heaven for you and pour down an overflowing blessing.**

John and Jean affixed the banner to the wooden panels on a Saturday night so it would be a sight to behold for the people who walked in on Sunday morning. It had its impact. The congregants had never been so visually confronted with the words of scripture.

At the opening of the service, John called attention to the banner and extended credit to Jean for its making. At the end, as folks were filing out, many complimented and thanked Jean. One comment that Pastor John would always remember came from an older lady: "I've done that kind of thing and I know it's a whole lot of work. It takes a bunch of dedication – and love. I'm so glad you're here and I know many other people are too." Another member said, "I never realized it was about God. Until I saw that banner, I thought we just gave to the church. I didn't know God is directly involved."

* * * * *

Yes, John ruminated that Sunday afternoon, do the basic stuff a pastor is supposed to do, and you'll be alright. Oh, there'd be times of strife when John challenged the congregation in various ways, but the love remained. God's grace always turned out to be sufficient.

Chapter 15

Vegetarian

When he embraced the Christian faith, John began contemplating vegetarianism. God certainly seemed to prefer it; early on God bestowed upon humans an exclusively fruit and vegetable diet. John desired to live as much as he could within God's preferences, but the meatless thing seemed to be too much to inflict on his family, too much religion at one time. His Christianity had already brought about substantial upheaval in their lifestyles.

Later one of John's children prompted the change. Just as younger daughter Ann led him back to church, older daughter Laura opened the way to vegetarianism. She came home from college one day and announced she had become a vegetarian. She didn't articulate her reasoning, but John felt it had its origin in her reading of Sinclair's *The Jungle*. So whenever Laura was home, they ate vegetarian. Following one of Laura's visits, as Jean and John were washing dishes, John observed, "You know, these vegetarian recipes Laura uses are really quite tasty. I like them." Jean was silent for a few moments, then said,

"Should we just be vegetarian all the time?" And thus it was done.

Books like Jonathan Foer's *Eating Animals* and Kathy Freston's *Veganist* further convinced John and Jean of the moral imperative. The rise of factory farming and the cruelty inherent in it and the slaughtering processes were facts they could not ignore. Similarly, knowledge of the contributions of beef production to deforestation and desertification and climate change reinforced their decision.

* * * * *

"Jean and I have decided to become vegetarian," John announced in connection with devotions at the ministerial association meeting. It was his first public declaration of the new discipline he was embracing.

"Whatever for?" one of the clergy inquired.

"I was hoping you'd ask that. In the beginning, God told the first people – the man and the woman – to eat plants. God didn't authorize meat eating until after the Fall and the Flood. Clearly eating animals was not a favored thing."

"Then why did he give us these?" another minister asked, pointing to his canines."

"Evolution," my dear Baptist friend. "Evolution. But to continue, it's clear, isn't it, that we won't be devouring flesh when God's kingdom comes in full? That just doesn't fit in with the wolf and lamb thing. And – most importantly – the Bible calls us to live – to the extent we can – as if the kingdom has already arrived, not just in part, but wholly."

Although the members of the association didn't necessarily agree with all the details of John's theology, they respected his interpretation and decision.

* * * * *

Then there was the problem of potlucks. People were sure to notice the pastor passing by the tantalizing meat dishes they had lovingly prepared. They deserved an explanation. John considered preaching on the subject, but decided that was maybe a too "in-your-face" approach. So he opted to use his newsletter column as the medium with which to communicate his and Jean's rationale for an animal-free diet.

Ted Fish, chair of the Staff-Parish Relations Committee, called the Monday morning following the Sunday on which the newsletter was distributed. "We've got a little issue going on, John. Can you come down?"

"Sure, Ted. Be there in a few minutes. Do I need to bring anything?"

"No. Nothing needed. See you soon."

"Mary, I'm going down the hill to see Ted Fish," John said to the church secretary as he walked out of his office. "If Ken Johnson comes in about the roof bids, tell him I should be back soon."

Well, at least Ted didn't sound upset, John thought as he drove down the hill, so hopefully it's nothing too serious. Once he and Ted got settled at Ted's kitchen table with cups of coffee, Ted got right to the point: "It's about your newsletter article."

"About being a vegetarian?"

"Yep. Kate Burns doesn't take too kindly to it. She hand-delivered a complaint to me. Says you should have to pay for the paper and ink used to print the article."

"And her reasoning?"

"She says you're just voicing your opinion and the church shouldn't have to bear the expense for you to do that."

"Oh."

"She also feels that you're biting the hand that feeds you. After all, this is an agricultural area, she points out, and it's farming that pays your salary."

"Sounds like I hit a nerve."

"Question is, should we take this to the committee?"

"I think so. Let's find out what they have to say."

* * * * *

John had to fight off his temptation to be angry at Kate. How dare she challenge his well-reasoned position? He wanted to reject her complaint out-of-hand as so much nonsense. Yet, frustrating as it was for him to admit, there was a lot about her to respect. She was smart. She was articulate. She was a woman who had overcome numerous obstacles to make something of her life. Widowed with small children, she went to the university and became a high school teacher. She closed out her career as a leader in vocational education. Now she was a lady farmer, overseeing the cultivation of several acreages.

Sitting in his car in Ted's driveway, John phoned the church office. "Hi, Mary. Has Ken Johnson come in?

"Nope. No sign of him?"

"I guess he got tied up in something else. He only said he 'might drop by.' I'm going to go into the city – get some lunch and do some hospital visits. See you tomorrow."

Driving alone in his car often helped John to relax from the tensions of the day. He was hoping that would be the case on this day. As he drove he thought of the time he and the family were in Beardstown, Illinois. The smell hit them hard. "What the devil is that horrible stink?" he asked no one in particular. "It smells like burning flesh, like death itself." Later he learned he wasn't wrong in his assessment. It was the smell of the slaughterhouse.

Next, the family's trip to the Rockies came to mind. They were driving through Kansas and encountered another pungent, awful, odor. They soon witnessed the source – a cattle confinement operation. "I'm never going to eat meat again," John said. Two hours later they pulled into a restaurant for lunch. John ordered the ribeye steak sandwich. So much for the meatless pledge.

His brain didn't register the brake lights soon enough. He pushed the brake pedal as hard as he could. The tires squealed as they went into the slide. Then the impact and the sounds of head and tail lights shattering and metal crunching. The driver of the car ahead was already heading his way by the time John processed what had happened.

"What the hell!" the man shouted. "Were you sleeping or what? What moron taught you to drive?"

John, now out of his car, responded with his own question. "Why did you stop like that?"

"Open your eyes, buddy," the man said and pointed to the deer lying on the other lane of the pavement. "Damn things aren't supposed to be out this time of day."

John walked over, put his hand up to stop oncoming traffic, and looked at the deer. She was alive and struggling to get up, but her rear legs were smashed. Her blood was flowing down the incline of the roadway. John looked into her eyes and saw the fear – the terror – there. She knew that death was reaching out for her and she wasn't ready.

The police came. John was ticketed. The deer was shot. He and the man exchanged insurance information. John got back in his car and drove toward the church, thinking of the look in that deer's eyes. He'd read that animals being led into the slaughterhouse know what's coming, that they can hear and smell the death, and now he knew that it was true. He thought of people and their pets and how the people grieved for any suffering the animals experienced; why couldn't they relate to the suffering their carnivore habits were visiting on so many innocent animals? "I guess," he mumbled to himself, "that it's the same as the way we ignore the suffering of strangers."

* * * * *

The committee was unanimously supportive of John. Morry Ore, the lay leader, jumped right on Kate's assertion that the article was merely John's opinion: "That's what we pay him for – to give us his considered opinions on the scriptures and how they call him – and us – to live now."

Thank you, God, for Morry, John prayed, for reasons beyond the immediate circumstances. Morry was a driving force in the congregation. He and his wife Shari were instrumental in calling the church to mission and through their zealous work, they had truly made a difference in many lives.

Ron Weaver, who had always considered himself a protector of Pastor John, weighed in with: "I don't agree with John's ideas here, but I know he's sincere and I support his effort to help us know God. He's been with Char and me in many difficult times and we love him and Jean like our own children.

Fay Jones, the choir director, unable to resist a dig at John, said, "Even though he can't sing, he's still close to God and I appreciate his courage to speak out. John, if you need a little break after all this, take my van and go somewhere with your family."

"This is really outrageous!" Peggy Larson exclaimed. "Do we want a pastor or a patsy leading our church? I know that Pastor John always has our church at the center of his thoughts. Our family, which, as you know, is substantial, supports him one hundred percent."

"Well," Ted said, "looks like we're in agreement. Who wants to draft a response to Kate's complaint?"

"I will," Morry volunteered.

John left the meeting humbled. He did not expect the enthusiastic support he'd received. Actually, he questioned whether he deserved it. Did he really, in his heart, love them as much as they expressed? Only God knew for sure. All he could do was try as hard as he could. As for Kate, she accepted the committee's decision with grace and said not another word about it.

After Word

Following his last sermon and a farewell celebration, Pastor John and Jean – with the help of many – loaded up the moving van, packed up the car, and set off down the road to California.

Somewhat like John Steinbeck in *Travels with Charley*, they wandered across the northern United States looking at America – exhausted but thrilled by what they encountered. People were kind, people were helpful. There was immense beauty, from the plains of Nebraska to the mountains of Wyoming and Montana. John wasn't sure he wanted to get to their destination; it was so good just to be *en route*.

As these words are written, their transplanted beings are seeking to root in the dry, dusty, rocky southern California soil. It's tough to root in such unaccustomed turf. Yet John and Jean's faith experience tells them that God waters even the driest of places, softening the earth so fruit can be borne.

The churches so feebly described in these pages represent the hope of the world. Through churches the way of Jesus – the way of life – is preached, taught, experienced, and lived out. That way is the way of kindness – kindness to family and kin, friends and enemies, acquaintances and strangers – kindness to the planet itself; it is the way of salvation.

Pastor John's ongoing prayer is for our churches to resist the temptations of isolation and to instead embrace the world with the Spirit of kindness, so that the world might be transformed.

Amen.

Made in the USA
Columbia, SC
15 October 2022

69416751R00091